BIG MAN WITH A SHOVEL

BIG MAN
WITH A
SHOVEL

Joe Amato

STEERAGE PRESS

Paperback edition (2020):
ISBN-10: 098363260X
ISBN-13: 978-0983632603

Kindle edition (2020):
ISBN-10: 0983632618
ISBN-13: 978-0983632610

Cover consultants: Nathalie op de Beeck, Maryanne Khan, and Michael Amato.

Thanks to John O'Brien, Michael Joyce, Frank Lentricchia, Tim Hunt, Andrew Levy, and Stephen Spotte for their encouragement and inspiration.

~ STEERAGE PRESS ~
Boulder, CO, and Normal, IL

for Kass Fleisher & Richard Powers

& for the little guy

CONTENTS

BIG MAN WITH A SHOVEL

Prologue

—Goddamn fucking machine.
—Yeah, and right when the shit is really coming down. Ain't that the way of it?
—Yeah. I thought Shorty had this fucker fixed.
—Me too.
—Boy am I gonna give him hell about this when we see him.
—I guess we'll have to clear these walkways the hard way then.
—Yeah.

~

—I hear you're thinkin' about college.
—I'm thinking about it.
—You oughtta go.
—You think so?
—Better than *this* bullshit. Or gettin' your nuts shot off.
—Yeah, maybe.
—No maybes about it. What does Frannie say?
—What do you think Frannie says?
—She's right, Joe. Leastways, I think so.
—Maybe.

~

–That about does it then?

–Yeah, but now we gotta go back over the front.

–Looks like there's another two-three inches since we started.

–Yeah, this shit is really comin' down.

–Man am I gonna give Shorty hell when we see him.

~

–Hey—you really put it to me and Wylie with that so-called repair job on the small blower.

–What?

–That fucking blower you supposedly fixed. Piece of shit went tits up on us yesterday over at the factory, right in the middle of a squall. All's it probably needed was a new spark plug.

–I never got to it.

–What do you mean you never got to it?

–I mean, Joe, that Red pulled me off it to tune up White's car.

–Fucking Red!

–Fuckin' Red? Fuckin' White, if you ask me, Joe.

–Fucking Red, White, black or fucking blue, t' fuck's the difference, Wylie? Either way, me and you busted our asses to shovel every fucking walkway at the factory.

–Jesus Christ but that just breaks my heart to hear that, boys. That just breaks my fuckin' heart.

–Fuck you, Shorty. That job took us four fucking hours. And with the shit coming down like there was no tomorrow.

–Am I correct in assuming that you two signed up to shovel snow on occasion?

–Fuck you, Shorty.

–If you're so pissed off, then why don't you guys take it up with Red? I'd pay good money to see that.

–Fuck you, Shorty.

–Take it up with Red, why dontcha?

–When we feel like havin' our balls broke, we'll let you know.

–I see, Wylie. Uh-huh.

–Fuck you.

–Fuck me, huh?

–That's right—fuck you, Shorty. What we do is our business.

–Yeah?—well what I do is get paid for my expertise. Which I got more of than you two grunts put together.

–Yeah? Well we left the blower for you in the back of the pickup, so why don't you scoot your ass on over there and see if you can put alla that so-called expertise of yours into changing a FUCKING spark plug.

~

–Red, Shorty here says that you pulled him offa the small blower to tune up White's car.

–Yeah, what of it?

–Well Joe and me, we were thinking that maybe it would help the operation—Atlas—if we had a better sense of priorities.

–A better set a what?

–A sense of priorities—you know, what's most important, what's least important, what we should work on first, second, and so on. Plus we think Mr. White would probably agree. The other day—

–Priorities?

–Yeah.

–Tell you what: why don't you two punks get your plow jockey asses back to work, and leave the priorities to me, OK?

–

–I said OK?

–Yeah.

–Yeah, OK Red.

~

–Gotta hand it to you two—at least you tried.

–Tried what, Shorty?

–Your two pals here, Charlie—they tried to talk Red into—what was it you said? Better priorities? Priorities, lord. I nearly pissed myself when I heard that come out of your mouth, Wylie.

–He's pulling my joint, right? You guys didn't approach Red.

–Take it easy, Charlie. We just figured it was worth a shot.

–What the fuck were you two assholes thinking? If there's one thing I know, I know I need that paycheck, and I know you guys need that paycheck, and I know I need guys I can work with. I ain't one for asskissing, but—

–Charlie's right, boys. I been working in this shithole nearly nine years, and I seen Red fire guys who had three-four years in without so much as blinking that pitch-black eye a his.

–Well I'll be a son of a bitch.

–How's that, Wylie?

–I'll be a son of a bitch. I don't know about you, Joe, but I'm touched, downright touched at this show of concern by our fellow man.

–I'm touched too, Wylie. Mighty touched.

–Yep, we're both touched, by god. Who woulda thunk you'd find so much brotherly love in a—how'd Charlie here put it?—in a shithole like this.

–You fuckin' guys are too much.

–Aw c'mon, Shorty, why don't you plant a big sloppy kiss right here on my cheek—here, this cheek—

–Jesus Christ, Wylie, I ain't seen an ass-cheek that smooth since Sally was a baby!

–Really? Well then how about you, Charlie? What say you bend down and plant those lips of yours—

–Save it, Wylie—you're not my type. And if there's one thing I know, I know what my type is.

~

–So what's bugging you about the big man?

–I don't know. Something.

–Like what?

–It's like he's holding something in.

–He lets go all right when he's working.

–Yeah, but something else.

–He's hiding something?

–I don't know.

–Well whatever it is, the guys have taken to givin' Red a hard time about things.

–Yeah?

–Yeah. Shorty told me that Lucas told Red—this is while the new guy was giving Lucas a hand unhitching the spreader—that we oughtta buy a new wrecker.

–Lucas said that?

–That's what Shorty tells me.

–Well—we oughtta buy a new wrecker.

–Fuckin'-A right we oughtta. Wanna half of this sandwich?

–No. What is it?

–Capicola.

–Mustard?

–Mayo.

–Mayo? What the hell—no, no thanks. Lucas. You tap the guy on the shoulder and he nearly shits his pants. What do you suppose got into him?

–I don't know, but just bein' around the new guy seems to be havin' that effect on the guys. What is it about him?

–I don't know. But Red doesn't seem to be afraid of him.

–No, he don't. You like the big man?

–Nothing not to like, far as I can see. Works hard, talks sense, is nothing if not friendly. You?

–He's OK I guess.

–You guess?

–Well it's just that I never known his kind—

–Oh don't start that shit again.

–Well, you said something was buggin' you about him.

–Yeah, but it's not like I don't trust him. It's nothing like that.

–Well, so you don't know something and I don't know something. We make a good pair, man.

–That we do, my friend.

What with the computer and all manner of automation, new heroes and anti-heroes have been added to Walt Whitman's old work anthem. The sound is no longer melodious. The desperation is unquiet.

Studs Terkel, *Working*

ACT I

The Man

1

Rome Apples

They can break you.

Editor's is a steady rumble, voiced over and under the real. She's the talk in my sleep these days. And she's there for a reason, she tells me: to set the record straight.

The exteriors seem to me always to have been cooling down, crystallizing, always a subdued brightness. There might have been two months of summer—green, humid summer hemmed in by a late spring and early fall. Everyone went a little mad during those two months or, if you were lucky, ten weeks. But by mid-September the sky would give way to a thick blanket of grey, and the winds would carry just enough chill to remind you that time was running out. The heavens were out of sight then, and heaven was out of the question.

There was the occasional reprieve, that warm spell in late fall some of us call Indian summer, a week or two of gentle breezes, hazy sun and moderate temperatures. But nothing was guaranteed. Like us, the Indians on the rez to the south—my mother's granddad, who died the day after I was born—could get one Indian summer, or two, or a premature bout of winter.

Judging by the look on her face, I would say Editor is pleased with my opener. Thinks it'll hook most readers. Would prefer that I didn't talk about *her*, though. At least, not yet. Says most readers will find her mere presence at this point something of a turn-off.

But if she's going to insist on intervening, then I'll insist on letting you know when she does.

It's raining. Hard. Editor steps out into the rain, measuring her insides against the outside, working inside out to let the outside in.

She's a real character, Editor—has a method, and the stomach for it.

~

The stomach for it: imagine that I'm a young man—which is to say, imagine that I'm not a senior citizen with a chronic case of arthritis in my right hand. Imagine there are no orange groves in sight. Imagine that I haven't a clue yet that a handful of months in 1965 will seat me at a keyboard pounding out drafts for twenty years, trying to account for what happened. Trying to get it right, to do justice to it.

Writing, or pretending to.

It's early in 1965, a small town about an hour's drive north-northeast from Syracuse, New York. We'll call it Mannville. We'll call it February of 1965 in Mannville, New York.

Editor is eyeing me carefully now.

No, I'm no writer, not really. Editor is the one with the chops. She's the talk in my sleep these days. Sometimes I let her call the shots, even when she's all wet.

They can break you, he tells me, repeating the words I overheard nearly forty years ago. Repeating the words that could have been addressed to me, but were not. Were not.

I follow his dictates, his dictation: *They can break you*, he tells me.

They can break you, kid.

~

Joe is a strong young guy, a little younger than me, but with a lot more on the ball. You can tell he isn't going to be stuck driving a plow and doing mule work all his life. But you can't tell if he has it in him to make something of himself.

–Working hard or hardly working, boys?

I'm standing in the middle of the sidewalk, leaning on my shovel, taking a drag off a Marlboro. Joe squats in front of the newspaper box, reading the headlines through the frosted glass. He's a reader, Joe is. It's Monday morning, it's half past nine, and we could both use a cup of mud and a jelly donut. But no time for that right now, so we're just taking a breather.

–Hey Mr. Colella, how's it hanging?
–OK. But this leg of mine—

He reaches down and pinches his left knee between his fat ungloved thumb and forefinger.

–this leg of mine is just murder when it's cold like this, JoJo.

Joe stands and tips his head at the newspaper box.

–Looks like we're bombing some bases.

Mr. Colella shakes his head.

–Things is gonna get worse before they get better, boys. Way of the world.
–That's what my old man says. Says this war is gonna heat up but good.

~

My old man never says that, Editor reminds me. That's just me, always trying to make small talk. Always trying too hard. My old man?—he could give a goddamn about Southeast Asia, me, my mother, anything outside of his six-pack a day and sauerkraut and sausages every Sunday.

He'll die before I'm thirty.

Mr. C looks at Joe, and smiles. Even at nineteen, Joe is one of those young guys you meet every once in a great while who have enough self-assurance for any five young guys. Comfortable in his own skin, I guess. Wish I could have been like him then, but it just wasn't in me. It just wasn't me.

Back then we were older and wiser than our youthful years, Joe and I and even Charlie. Ours was a generation that had felt its coming of age, and was keenly aware of the passing of time. We were impatient, some of us, even a little angry, because we knew that, life being what life tends to be, disappointment was just around the corner. And we didn't want *anyone* telling us to get in line and take it like a man. We'd seen how that had played out in our folks. We may have been old souls, many of us, but they were old before their time. The war had probably done that to them. But the early onset of adulthood in their lives had made it easier for us to see in them what they *might* have been. And most of them knew this in fact, figured their kids would go one better as a result.

So to say that an aura of possibility loomed during those years isn't just hype. We saw ourselves, some of us, as instruments of change, within and without. Our only mistake, most of us, was that we didn't reach far enough, or didn't last the stretch. Sometimes it just can't be helped. And sometimes—sometimes you reach too far.

Editor frowns, advising against the *didactic. It's been done to death*, she says. Appreciates the cultural *platitudes* not a whit. Wants me to just *get on with it, and without the exposition.* Says I should *stop explaining. Unless you're some kind of avant-garde funnyman*, she blathers, *the adage is "show, don't tell."* Adds, insult to injury, *you've got your history all wrong, besides.* Says the Me Generation had promise, but just never learned the value, *the necessity of discipline, of self-restraint.* Never learned the *generative sacrifice.*

But readers need a few handholds, I say, especially with some difficult terrain in the offing. And what's all this about avant-garde funnymen? Even James, that dramatizing scold, did his share of showing *and* telling.

If I had to write the way she wants me to, I'd blow my brains out.

So fuck her, is what I say. And as far as history goes, she voted for Nader, so what the fuck does she know about history.

Yeah, sure—the majority of us, like the majority of most generations, will take it like a man and watch the clock tick off our losses. What of it?

But Joe—JoJo, as his folks and all the older folks in town call him—Joe might turn out to be the kind of guy who'll show some of us what to do with our anger.

Or not. You just can't say, life being what life tends to be.

For some, Joe is a mystery, and one worth plumbing. A few of our teachers in high school. Women, one young woman in particular. For others, Joe is a threat to the system, a troublemaker. Most of our teachers. Our boss. It's not in what he does or says, you understand—it's in what he *doesn't* do or say. He never chokes up in the face of authority, never skips a beat.

Never.

Mystery or threat, Joe is someone you pursue.

~

–How's your mother holding up, JoJo?
–She's doing OK.
–That's good to hear. I miss that old man of yours.
–Yeah.

The shops are opening soon and we still have the other side of Main Street to clear. But first we've got to spread some salt-sand mix on this side. So I give Joe a nudge—I'm the straw boss on this job because I have seniority. Only by two months, but two months is two months.

–What say we get back to work, huh Joe?
–Yeah, we better.
–JoJo—you stopping by the house later tonight?
–Can't, Mr. Colella. Working a double today.
–Oh boy. Should I tell Frannie you'll phone?
–Yeah, thanks.
–Pace yourselves, boys, pace yourselves.

We scoop the mix from the wheelbarrow with our shovels and toss it across the sidewalk. Doesn't take us long to cover the entire length. Then we walk to the other side of the street and begin clearing the way, pushing the snow off toward the gutter. Joe is right-handed and I'm a southpaw, which works out well because we can shovel facing each other, without one of us having to look over his shoulder to check with the other guy. We work well together, especially when we're humping the heavy wet shit we'll be seeing in a month or so. Right now it's three-four inches of fluff, with a slick layer of ice underneath. Easy work, but even here you gotta pay attention, watch your footing.

You've got to, corrects Editor, ever the author.

Whatever.

We finish up, throw the shovels and the barrow in the bed of the Ford, and head back to the garage, a few merchants waving at us through their store windows. I'm driving, Joe is lost in thought, as usual. I know better than to try to ~~shoot the shit~~

Editor doesn't like this—says it's out of character.

OK then.

I know better than to try to converse with him this early in the morning, so I flip on the radio, light another Marlboro, and crack open the window. I'm driving slow so as not to risk nicking anything with my plow. Mannville's streets are narrow, and the townspeople are stubbornly opposed to alternate parking. It's a small town that wants to stay small.

~

Atlas is a large regional contractor headquartered in Mannville, with branches in three counties. We handle snow removal for local businesses, churches, hospitals, and factories. If the factory is unionized, Atlas pays off the union and brings in its own men. When it's really coming down we even help the county crews plow the main thoroughfares. It's good public relations.

The owner, Mr. White, makes a bundle during winters, and works a skeleton crew summers just to keep us on the payroll. Training new men is expensive, and Mr. White knows it. So Joe and Charlie and I do mowing and landscaping, and sweep and stripe parking lots with Atlas's antiquated equipment. From the outside, Mr. White is a canny businessman who cares about his customers. From the inside, he's a skinflint who'll work you to death if you give him half the chance.

But I bet you knew that already, right?

Always happy to be of service, goes the Atlas motto. It's painted in orange cursive on the side of our white pickup, next to a miniature of a chubby man with a shovel, smiling.

Editor reminds me that the chubby little man with a shovel resembles Mr. White. At least, Joe and I think so. Charlie doesn't, but Charlie never agrees with anybody about anything.

~

We pull into the Atlas lot next to a large pile of mix with a tarp over it. The mustard-yellow front loader is parked directly in front of the pile, its massive shovel resting on the frozen ground. The wrecker is pulled up to the closest bay, facing the garage, and the spreader attached to the back of our big plow-dump truck juts out from the far side of the building, the truck itself blocking passage around that side. A large sign above the all-white garage duplicates the image on our pickup. The garage is attached on the backside to a newer prefab structure that we call the warehouse, five thousand square feet stocked with parts and supplies, with overhead doors around back for unloading.

By the time we walk through the front door of the garage, it's nearly eleven. Mr. White's pristine black Imperial is parked in the far bay, where he always keeps it in the winter. The inside of the garage is poorly lit, and reeks of bad coffee and bearing grease and sweat. The garage has four bays, two with lifts; two large roll-aways stuffed with hand tools; an acetylene welding outfit; two wash sinks; a tire machine; three oil drums; two long work benches at the back; three coiled lead lamps dangling from above; assorted tire irons. You get the picture. Everything looks a little worse for wear—even the roll-aways, which belong to the mechanics. A beat-up table radio sits atop one of the benches, volume turned way down, hissing out AM hits.

The ambience, if you can call it that, is one of men working harder than they want to be working, than they should be working. And for less than they should be making. You can feel it, if you can feel anything, but it's tough to put your finger on just what you're feeling. The grime? The disarray? Or simply the structure itself, the contrast between its surfaces and its interiors? The few customers who drop by on occasion are always a bit surprised to see how cheery, upstanding Mr. White tends shop. At least today, for a change, the overhead heaters are keeping it above fifty degrees.

Red is on us before the door shuts behind me.

—So, the fuck-off artists are finally back.

Red's a stocky guy about my height with "Semper fi" tattooed on his left forearm and a patch over his right eye. He's usually got a Chesterfield hanging from his mouth. We've learned the hard way not to respond to Red's baiting. As Mr. White's number one slave driver, he can make your life plain miserable. And on a job like this, how much misery you're willing to put up with becomes strictly a matter of how much you *can* put up with. We're not talking about one's capacity for giving and taking a little grief, no. Keeping your mouth shut around here means you know you can put up with only so much backbreaking *misery*. Keeping your mouth shut around here means you're willing to stick around, to *last*.

Red walks into the office, and we head for the coffee stand in the back corner of the garage, hoping we're not too late to split a donut. The rest of the crew is leaning against a pickup parked in the nearest bay, its hood up. There's Shorty, our lead mechanic, and next to him Carl and Gus, our heavy equipment operators. Lucas, our other mechanic, has called in sick.

We can tell by the shit-eating grins on their faces that we're too late.

–Shit.
–Yeah.

A roar of laughter, and we turn to see the three splitting their guts.

–Fuckin pigs.

This just makes them laugh harder. Joe shakes his head, grabs a cup of mud black as night. I do the same, take a sip, and add an extra quarter-cup of Cremora. We join the crew.

–I know it was you you fuckin pig, Shorty.

Shorty's in his mid-thirties. Potbelly, but sturdy. Nice guy, real family man. Sweet wife, two kids, and a Dalmatian puppy. I've seen him put away half a dozen glazed without blinking an eye.

–Fuck you short-timer.
–Being an old-timer doesn't win you any medals.

Nice guy, like I say, but he really gets my goat.

~

Editor is beginning to grow impatient with me. Doesn't think I can possibly recall lines of dialogue with any precision, would rather I reduce exchange to a minimum, and narrate the general contours of place and character, thus steering clear of the sort of phony literary realism that the Hemingway and Carver tribes have popularized. (I'm paraphrasing.) Editor doubles as dialogue coach sometimes, so she may be on to something for a change.

~

–Where's Charlie?
–Where else, Joe. In the shithouse. Another long night.

Just then Charlie walks in the front door, shivering from the cold and white as a sheet.

–Long night, Charlie?
–What's it to you, Carl?
–Well, I'm just concerned, as a friend. You look like you might have left your asshole in the toilet, along with the rest of your shit.
–Fuck you Carl, you gimp bastard. If there's one thing I know, I know a gimp bastard when I see one.

We all laugh, even Carl. We take turns serving as targets for one another, and now the bulls-eye is painted on Charlie's back. Livens up the workday, gives us something to look forward to.

But before Charlie and Carl can really get into it, Red's arm pushes open the office door, and Mr. White walks out, Red trailing. Mr. White is a pear-shaped man in his mid-fifties, fair complexion—but artificially tanned—dressed in a white shirt, red-and-blue-striped tie, black wool trousers, Florsheims, and a black fedora. Always appears to be about to give a speech. Reminds me of that guy who played the judge in *Miracle on 34th Street*. Whose daughter played the perfect mom for a spell in *Lassie*.

Looked it up: Gene Lockhart.

Editor winces.

Mr. White clears his throat, does his best to look us straight in the eye, but keeps glancing down at the concrete floor as he speaks.

–Listen up, men: looks like there may be a blizzard in the making, possibly as early as tomorrow morning. If it hits, weather forecasters are saying we could get as much as three feet. Depends on the wind.

We all groan. At this time of year, *if it hits* almost always means *when it hits*, and the only question is how much will drop on us from the lake to the west. None of us thinks to ask, though, because whether the storm dumps three inches or three feet, whether the prevailing winds blow northwesterly or swirl around from the east, we've got to be prepared for the worst. And this translates to more work for us—the vehicles have to be gassed up, mix has to be loaded in advance. But most important from our point of view, we've got to be at the garage an hour earlier than usual, ready to roll. That makes it 5 AM.

–I've, uh, instructed Red to bring in an extra laborer from our Rome branch. He'll be here tonight, and he's going to be with us for, oh, perhaps for the rest of the season.

Now we're even less pleased. But we know better than to object. Mr. White has done the math—not too much snow so far this season, but it's been a cold winter, and he knows that paying us time-and-a-half to spread salt all over town is beginning to add up. Better to bring in another guy at a buck-and-a-half an hour than to pay Joe and Charlie and me two-and-a-quarter for every hour we work over forty.

The moment the office door shuts behind Mr. White, Red puts on his war face. Mr. White may make the laws in this ~~chickenshit~~ operation, but Red enforces them, sometimes at the top of his lungs, but often, like now, in a snarling whisper.

–OK you cocksuckers, time to get the lead out of your asses and earn a living for a change. No more overtime for you pussies, no sir, not for *you* pussies.

Red is tipping his head in Charlie's direction as he aspirates that last put-down. We all try to ignore him, but as I pull my knit cap on over my ears, I catch Shorty bouncing a tire iron off of his left palm a couple of times, like he's weighing the pleasure of treating Red's skull to a few good whacks.

Shorty has done some time—bar brawl—so he knows what he'd be in for, but his family needs that paycheck. Really needs it. And besides, Red looks to have one thick skull on him. If Shorty didn't do the job good and proper like, he might have more on his hands than even he bargained for.

Red stares at Shorty for a moment, then flicks his cigarette on the garage floor at our feet, exiting into the office.

Joe and Charlie and I head out the door with Gus, who's on his way to the loader. The wind has already picked up and a few flakes have started blowing around. The clouds seem a notch lower and a shade darker than an hour ago. Even with a cup of mud in your gut and four layers on, your stomach muscles tighten against it.

–What's with this Rome guy, Gus—you know anything about him?
–Nope. All's I know is you gotta watch yourself with them Rome boys. Some of 'em are bad apples—really bad. Connected.
–Connected? But we're an open shop—ain't no dues to shake down. Why the hell would they come sniffing around here?
–It's not about shakedowns, Charlie—even the unions ain't got enough work for alla them boys. So every now and then one'll fall a little far from the tree.
–So, what, so we gotta treat this guy with kid gloves?
–You just gotta be careful is all. I heard about this one guy, foreman over at Butch's a coupla years ago, who gave this temp kid—
–Temp?
–Yeah, they hire extra guys during the summers, when it's busy. It's a union shop, a-course.
–Yeah, so?
–So this guy, he was givin' this kid a hard time yknow, tellin' him he was fuckin' up but good loadin' the trucks. And a few nights later this guy, he ended up with company over t' his house.

–Company?
–Yeah, and not from the local. There were three of 'em. This guy's wife—one of 'em poked a twelve-gauge between her legs with their kids lookin' on, and that ended that.
Charlie seems to go silent at this last, but I'm not about to let it lay.

–Whatsamatter, Charlie?—a little too close for comfort?
–You wish.

Charlie pauses, then continues.

–If there's one thing I know, I know what a close shave is. And that ain't what I call a close *shave*.

She winks at me at this last. That Charlie. Even Editor has taken a liking to her.

2

Second Shift

The night goes and does not go as expected.

First, after Joe and Wylie and Charlie finish plowing Singerman's (closed on Mondays) and re-salting the walkways at both branches of Merchant Savings and Loan, they have supper together—Charlie prefers to call it dinner—at Ruby's Diner. Joe orders his cheeseburger and fries, Wylie his bowl of chicken soup and BLT on rye, and Charlie her house salad with blue cheese dressing followed by her weekly serving of liver and onions. Joe and Wylie drink Cokes, Charlie orders a root beer.

The three take turns complaining about how little sleep they'll be getting—working a double shift, hitting the sack late, and having to be in an hour early the next morning. Charlie complains about her Aunt Liz, who has been giving her a difficult time of late for dropping off her five-year-old, Sally, so frequently. Joe and Wylie do their best to commiserate, knowing nothing firsthand of this sort of responsibility. Charlie wants to order a piece of coconut cream pie for dessert, but Wylie taps his watch to let her know that there won't be time. Joe and Wylie order coffees to go, Charlie a vanilla shake.

It's Wylie's turn to pick up the check. He leaves a healthy tip.

By 5:30 PM the local news stations are reporting that a fine powdery snow has begun to accumulate on the outskirts of town. The wind, which had been gusting just a few hours earlier, has momentarily died down, and the town itself is strangely quiet as the three head back to the garage for their night shift. The streets glisten under the streetlights with a thin coating of ice, and a flake or two falls as if in anticipation of the coming barrage while the Atlas pickup maneuvers slowly around town. But driver and passengers alike seem oblivious to such nuances of climate and mood. Wylie teases Charlie—again—asking whether she can really be "riding faggot" in light of the fact that she has "no balls." In return, Charlie regales Wylie with a colorful string of four-letter words, including two or three novel combination nouns and a fanciful gerund, "asshole-gazing." Joe smiles, keeping his eye on the road. All of this is standard operating procedure.

When they turn into the Atlas lot, they pull up alongside a vehicle they haven't seen parked there before—a white 1963 Oldsmobile station wagon in near-mint condition. Wylie ventures that it probably belongs to the "bad apple" from Rome, but Charlie disagrees, asserting that "no jamoke willing to make the trek up from that one-horse burg at this time of night would be driving a choice family man's wagon—a hog in the summertime, maybe, and a rat in the winter, sure, but never a wagon." Wylie objects both to the characterization of the "jamoke" in question as necessarily a bachelor, to the vehicle as necessarily a bachelor's vehicle, and to Rome as a "one-horse burg," accusing Charlie of a "downstate bias" owing to her "Bronx loser roots." Charlie begins her vehement rebuttal with "If there's one thing I know...."

This form of interaction, if not distraction, is, again, in keeping with the personal business typically conducted by our trio.

Editor at your service. Our M. Wylie has taken a break from the project at hand, and sends his regrets. In his absence, he has ceded us authority to relate the present episode, and several other abbreviated episodes, as we see fit. This M. Wylie ordinarily would not do, but he is in something of a rush on this project and working under considerable duress, as should become clear in later installments.

M. Wylie's previous divagations notwithstanding, it is our intention to narrate chapter and verse, but chapter and verse only. Point of view will, in the main, follow from the facts, rather than lead the facts astray, which may require a different species of attention than you have thus far been called upon to provide. For that matter, readers would be well advised to keep in mind that the true—"that [which] is fitted or formed or that functions accurately" (I cite from entry 5a under "true" in *Merriam-Webster's Collegiate*, 11th edition)—often requires for its elaboration the application of indirect agency.

For the record, our chief reservation in foregrounding a narrational agenda, as it were—whether M. Wylie's or our own, *here*—arises from our concern that disruptions of the sort evidenced in this and the prior two paragraphs, as well as in M. Wylie's (habitually) reflexive meandering in chapter 1, risk a certain gimmickry that threatens to undo that interdependence of fact and fiction upon which even unconventional narratives must occasionally rely in order to hold the attention of their readers. Though we would not deny those pleasurable effects thought by today's doctrinaires of text to inhere in the reading activity, reading nonetheless is, or should be, *serious business*, the judicious application of one's imaginative faculty to another's imaginative making in order to place the human condition under the alternately harsher and softer lights of intellect. Thus for a narrator to intrude compulsively upon his narration is, in our view, to hazard bookish flatulence. That the tale at hand is based on fact complicates purely fictive motives, to be sure, and renders moot what M. Melville postulated, not without some irony, as "the symmetry of form attainable in pure fiction." (See his conclusion to "Billy Budd, Sailor.")

Nevertheless, our presence here, and M. Wylie's there, must be accounted for, *if* we are to persist in being of two minds; thus some degree of (voiced) antagonism is, in truth, unavoidable. We trust our tale will suffer little, in any case, from this irregular discrepancy of teller, if not telling, and we thank you in advance for your indulgence here and elsewhere. Continuing, then, with our exposition:

Joe, Wylie and Charlie enter the garage with Charlie's rebuttal still hanging in the air, but all three are caught up short as their eyes fix instantly on a large figure dressed in dark overalls and a knit cap and leaning against one of the workbenches at the back, arms crossed in front of its chest. *It must certainly be a man*, but as only half of the fluorescent fixtures are kept on at this time of night—the mechanics are on twenty-four-hour call in case of emergencies—odd shadows fall across the figure, making it difficult to discern its features.

But it must certainly be a man: to this insight our three comrades instinctively, even desperately cling, for all three are filled to varying degrees with a vague sense of apprehension. The figure seems already, by its simple presence in the garage, to have effected a change in its surroundings of elemental proportions, throwing into stark relief the dispiriting quality of a meager workplace attendant to a low-wage job—which quality had, until this moment, been a matter at most of tacit knowledge. With the mysterious figure present, the workplace gloom is now, in a word, palpable.

For reasons he will be unable to explain later, Joe is somehow drawn to peer even more closely. He takes two short, hesitant steps toward the figure, noticing as he advances the massive iron shovel standing vertically beside, edge upon the concrete, long oak handle propped against the bench. The man-figure remains motionless and inarticulate.

Just then Red enters the garage from the office, clipboard in hand, Buster tagging along behind. Buster is the part-time handyman who takes care of garage maintenance—plumbing, lighting, heating, and the like—during evening hours. He's also Red's brother-in-law, and ever eager to do Red's bidding. The "spy" (our trio's favorite appellation for their honcho's sidekick) has evidently been thrown off his game, to judge by Buster's nervous glances in the direction of the man-figure. But Red, for his part, exhibits the absolute zero of perceptible anxiety.

Looking down at his clipboard but addressing himself to our trio, Red mutters "about goddamn time you're back," and then informs the three—or four—that the night watchman at the baby food factory, the chief employer in town and Atlas's largest single contract, has called to say it's snowing there, hard. Red barks at Wylie to help Charlie load the small blower onto one of the pickups. Charlie and Wylie are to drive the pickup and the dump out to the plant, where Carl is already standing by with the loader. Wylie will help Carl plow, then salt the lot, and Charlie will meantime clear the large walkways with the blower, well suited to smoothly paved, unobstructed surfaces with adjoining lawn areas, where the snow can be thrown. Once the plant lot and walkways are clear, Wylie and Charlie are to head over to the hospital with the pickup, then to the high school, and return finally to the factory lot to give Carl a hand as necessary. This will be the routine until the morning, when the second crew takes over. If too much snow accumulates to plow it up against the fence that surrounds the parking lot, Wylie will unhitch the spreader and use the dump to truck snow out of the lot to the open field on the east end of the plant.

Wylie and Charlie pat Joe on the back as they leave the garage, Charlie whispering "pace yourself" to Joe on her way out the door. Red takes note of Charlie's gesture, and scowls. But with Wylie and Charlie helping Carl, this leaves Joe and the man-figure, motionless throughout Red's instructions, to do the work originally intended for three men. To wit:

Every few weeks, Atlas will get a call from the Battaglia Rail Maintenance and Construction Company, asking for manpower to help clear the rail spurs that lead in and out of various municipal and private concerns—the power plant, the lumber yard and building supply company, the baby food factory. Clearing spurs is backbreaking labor—strictly shovel work, typically for teams of six men who'll trudge out to each end of a spur to struggle in threes with the hardened snow. "Mule work," as Red likes to call it, clearly pleased to have mules working under him.

Red now turns his attention to Joe and the man-figure—or rather, Red addresses only Joe directly, which is Red's customary way of treating temp workers. He growls at Joe to drive to the power plant with "it"— he tips his head at the man-figure without shifting his attention from Joe—where the two will be joined by a crew of Battaglia's men. He reminds Joe that Atlas is the subcontractor on this job, and that he's to take orders from the Battaglia crew chief. Joe simply nods.

After jotting down the various work assignments on his clipboard, Red returns to the office, glancing for the first time, and only for an instant, in the direction of the obscure, speechless figure, its arms still crossed in front of its chest. Joe, finding himself suddenly alone with the figure, manages to break the awkward silence by uttering a halfhearted "c'mon." The figure stands erect, grabbing the oak handle of the shovel with its left hand and, in one swift, effortless movement, swinging the massive implement over its left shoulder. As the figure steps forward, a beam of light falls directly on its face, confirming that the figure is, *as it must certainly be*, a man.

Relieved that the stoic figure is a man, but not yet knowing what to make of such a man, Joe turns toward the door, zipping his jacket and doing his best not to reveal any unease. And so a white man and a black man walk out into the cold together, which is where our story really begins.

3

Slush Pile

That night, as would typically happen after a long day of reading, her sleep was punctuated by the stubborn persistence of those pages upon which she had lavished such careful and astute attention. Her dreaming mind recombined the plots, voicings, images and imaginings of a dozen different writers, and even as she was dreaming she was somehow aware that this disrupted sleep would produce a useful end product: only writing of real value would be with her in the morning. Sleep was, in effect, her night shift.

And yet her work had become no more, if no less, than a job, and if she continued to love reading for its own sake, she also loved her job now not in spite of, but *because of* the standard of living it provided. And it provided, by any objective standard, a life well above the mean. Her reputation as the most tough-minded and conscientious of Kletterkraft's editorial staff was in any case well earned. She had consistently sought, in reviewing for publication both solicited and over-the-transom manuscripts, not simply to distinguish between the bad and the competent, the competent and the good, the good and the great; but to discern whether (her personal preference for what Metcalf had called a "dirt-prose" aside) a given submission managed to make a lasting mark on the consciousness of its reader, and thus, on the consciousness of its age.

She refused to relegate even unsolicited manuscripts to her interns exclusively—unheard of for a redactor of her status—making her less popular among the latter group than she might otherwise have been. Both in theory and in practice she refused to presume herself a mere "Kletterkraft customer," as the marketing branch was fond of describing its base. She chafed at the idea that publications must cater to a preconceived notion of readership; she disparaged newer, trend-driven policies that, in her view, had served to cultivate in her colleagues an apparatchik approach to the arts; and yet she regarded herself neither as a guardian of public taste nor as an arbiter of literary value *per se*. Rather, she viewed herself simply, if crucially, as a go-between responsible for locating and promoting exceptional writing. And she was fiercely committed to her selections, believing that her very integrity resided in her painstakingly diligent appraisals. Her summary reports on the merits of work she had recommended for publication were models of their kind—precise, thorough, perceptive.

Unfortunately, as a consequence of her proclivity for lending at every opportunity her fervent voice to her ardent convictions—"in the name of integrity," as she assured herself and everyone within earshot—her office mates had come to employ the standard sobriquet that workers often employ when forced to suffer an unyielding presence: throughout the office, and in adjoining firms located on the tenth floor with Kletterkraft, she was known simply as "the pain in the ass"—a development of which the pain in the ass was, happily for her sake, completely unaware.

But of late she too had sensed that her scrupulous editorial logic had left something to be desired, something crucial to her role as senior editor. Within weeks of her initial apprehension, and independently of any outside intervention, she arrived at the realization that her life's work was fundamentally *lacking*, that she had unearthed, finally, only a modest quotient of lasting talent.

Or so it seemed to her of late. Not even the most notable of her finds had gone on to achieve lasting success here or abroad, and while she understood only too well how fickle was literary celebrity—and despite her stated contempt for the award circuit, that "marketplace of manufactured merit"—she nevertheless took little comfort in the fact that her years of dedication had produced but a handful of known quantities, quantities known, as they customarily are, solely by that selfsame manufactured meritocracy.

And so she had come to appreciate her life's work as much for its material incentives as for its deeply felt ambitions: the good glass of wine every evening; the exorbitant if absolutely essential shopping spree; and especially, the annual June retreat to Paris, highlighted by the *Fête de la Musique* that she had so enjoyed as a child.

But on that night, after the autumn submission period had elapsed and she found herself once again knee-deep in mailings, one unsolicited piece in particular seemed to figure most prominently in her unconscious sampling. The manuscript copy itself was a slick, professional, PDF document. The story was set in the postwar world of the underclasses, and she had grasped on a first read that its *tranche de vie* qualities in essence troubled an old, indeed ancient distinction, that of legend versus history. It was unclear to her whether the author of the piece, a M. A_____, was steeped in the tradition as such— from experience she knew that great writing is occasionally produced by idiot savants—but the piece brought to our dreamer's restless sleep half-memories of Auerbach's *Mimesis*, his opening chapter on "Odysseus' Scar," a discussion that had taken hold of her critical imagination decades prior, while she was an undergraduate majoring in English at B_____.

But there was something else about the piece, too, something that pressed upon her professional self with far more urgency than questions of content or form: she felt that she had read the story someplace before.

The next morning she lingered in bed scouring her memory, unable to pinpoint exactly what it was about the narrative that felt so strangely familiar. After a light breakfast of dark coffee and a single slice of rye toast, she seated herself at her laptop—these days a recurring fixture on her dinner table—her fingers poised in anticipation above the keyboard as the screen brightened. Once at her favorite search engine, she typed in the title of the piece in question, which led her quickly to the following lines:

> I know him for a shovel man,
> A dago working for a dollar six bits a day

Not it, she thought, wincing at first at Sandburg's romantic treatment of the "dago" laborer, but then recalling that Sandburg had written the poem during the first World War, when Italian immigration was peaking. Perhaps we might forgive a nearly forty-year-old midwesterner of nineteenth-century origins his ethnic trespasses?

Perhaps not.

She next typed in a combination of key nouns relating to the story, and in two clicks of her mouse a 3" x 3" color photo appeared on her screen, below which the caption, "Man with snow shovel, standing by snowy woods on winter day"—apparently a stock photography site. Another combination of nouns, this one including "legend," brought her to *The Red Indian Fairy Book*, published by Frances Jenkins Olcott in 1917; she found herself reading Olcott's short entry entitled, "The Snow Man." *Dammit*, she whispered to herself, clicking back to her search engine to insert "myth" for "legend," which turned up the "nine Eskimo words for *snow*" just as "history" for "myth" brought her to "Have Snow Shovel, Will Travel: A History of Snow Removal," published by the National Snow and Ice Data Center (NSIDC). This was the first she'd heard of NSIDC, "supporting cryospheric research since 1976." Subsequent entries turned up links to snow shovel wholesalers and retailers, snow shoe outlets, jokes about snow shoveling, Snow White, snow leopards, environmental myths about snow (snow "makes some things warm") and of course, Wallace Stevens's famous poem, as well as the odd reference to the Norse god of thunder.

The Web had, for once, failed her. And a long Saturday afternoon of rummaging through her *Brewer's*, her *Bartlett's*, her *Britannica*, her entire home reference library produced similarly dismal results.

She was stumped, and would have to dig deeper still if she hoped to resolve this matter. But how, aside perhaps from teasing it out of the author, this M. A_____? And if she couldn't accept the piece for publication without first confirming its authenticity, she couldn't contact the author to inquire even casually into this matter of authenticity without first accepting the piece for publication. Company policy had long since prohibited any such inquiry between author and editor prior to a signed contract, a shrewd strategy that had all but eliminated legal disputes resulting from misunderstandings, willful or otherwise.

Though stuck in this editorial double bind, our senior editor had not thought—until now anyway—to avail herself of an obvious resource: her colleagues' expertise. Her general reluctance to do so in the past had stemmed not from some exaggerated sense of propriety or a desire on her part to maintain self-esteem. The plain and simple fact of the matter was that she had never successfully managed the transition to team player, not least because what had drawn her initially to her chosen profession was its promise of relative autonomy. At least, eventually. Eventually, her editorial judgments would be *her* judgments, untainted by force of argument or the need to compromise.

Still, her inquiries having proved insufficient to the task at hand—"a straightforward but nontrivial bit of textual sleuthing," she repeated to herself as if prepping for a pitch session—it occurred to her that there was one coworker who might offer some assistance, a junior editor who had struck her for some time now as earnest and competent, if sporadically jejune. Under the circumstances, contacting a junior person on a weekend could hardly appear out of bounds; and after all, this *was* the season of overtime pay for clerical workers, of deadlines pushed back, of going that extra mile. At any rate, it seemed to her that the current impasse was as good an excuse as any for testing the teamwork proposition, while affording her the opportunity to pursue what to her way of thinking would be a new mode of interaction.

~

Even before the knock on the door, Perkins was standing in the entranceway to her apartment preparing herself for this unanticipated visit. She waited two or three seconds after the knock, composed himself a final time, and pulled open the door casually, smiling as wide as she was able.

–Madeleine, hello!
–Greetings, Ms. Perkins.

The two women shook hands vigorously, intuiting each in her way that for this to be a cordial encounter, it must be anything but intimate. Madeleine's way, however, was never without its formalities, and it was not lost on Perkins, as she was known affectionately to her coworkers, that Madeleine—who insisted on being addressed simply as Madeleine—had affixed the two-letter title to ensure that the tenor of the evening would pick up where the tenth floor left off.

Pain in the ass, thought Perkins, smiling even wider.

–Can I get you something to drink? A glass of wine maybe, or—
–Black tea, if you have it. Where shall I put this?

Madeleine held up the black briefcase slung over her shoulder.

–Over here would be fine.

Madeleine placed the briefcase on the square marble coffee table. Marble seemed to her an odd choice for a single woman living in such tight quarters, and as she surveyed the scene, she noted that the grey hues did little to help the deep reds and browns of the futon cover. Perkins exited the living room/bedroom and busied herself making tea in the tiny kitchen, while pouring a glass of Chardonnay for herself. She downed one glass and poured another before the water came to a boil, cursing under her breath as the teapot wheezed. Madeleine meantime browsed the four makeshift bookshelves lining the walls of the tiny room, silently dismissing the majority of titles as *popular*.

–Honey and half-and-half OK?
–Just honey, thank you.

Perkins entered the living with a green plastic tray that held the steeping mug of tea, the honey, a spoon, the wineglass, the wine bottle, and several colorful napkins. She placed the tray on one corner of the marble square, and sat in the worn armchair—worn but serviceable, concluded Madeleine—at one end of and at right angles to the futon. Madeleine sat on the futon just within reach of her teacup. Perkins reached for her wineglass, then sat upright, crossing her legs in lotus position. She was wearing a blue knit top, khakis, argyle socks, and gold hoop earrings. Madeleine was dressed strictly on-the-job: navy suit, matching pumps, gold studs. The two women were exactly one generation apart in age, and demeanor.

Madeleine stretched for the mug and spoon, placing the mug on the table. With her spoon—mid-market flatware, in her estimation—she squeezed the tea bag against the side of the mug, a nasty habit, as her mother would say, that she hadn't been able to break. Using the spoon, she lifted the tea bag from the mug without thinking what she would do with it next. Perkins reacted quickly, unfolding her legs to stand, then leaning to grab with her free hand a napkin, then the honey, placing both before Madeleine.

–Don't worry—you can't hurt marble. It's a relic from an old relationship.

Madeleine dropped the steaming tea bag onto the napkin, which immediately soaked through to the marble. She frowned ever so slightly at the sight of the soaked, steaming napkin—or at least, this is how Perkins would later tell the story—then added a dollop of honey to her tea, then stirred—the spoon ended up on the napkin as well— then finally took a sip of tea, her face registering not one jot of satisfaction or dissatisfaction (as the tale would later circulate throughout the tenth floor). She cradled the mug in her hands as she spoke.

–Well. I suppose we should begin. I've brought the manuscript along, as we discussed last night.

She tipped her head at the briefcase. Perkins was careful to refrain from appearing too eager.

–May I?

Madeleine nodded, and Perkins placed her wineglass on the table, lifted the briefcase, opened it, and removed the hundred-odd page manuscript.

–Mind if I—
–Do, by all means.

Madeleine glanced out the window to see the crescent moon setting between two high-rise apartment buildings. Perkins leaned back in her chair and began to read the manuscript. The two women sat together in silence, one a junior editor and the other a senior editor, one reading and the other observing, one woman sipping too-cold white wine and the other sipping too-hot black tea, one a black woman and the other a white pain in the ass.

4

Revelations

Toro builds the first walk-behind snowblower in 1951. They're an infrequent but not unusual sight in northern regions of the US in the mid-sixties, around the time snowmobiles begin to gain in popularity.

A landscape shapes its noise, its circulations. Movers and shakers are themselves to be moved and shaken.

Should you find yourself behind the eight ball, *making it* comes first.

And once you've made it, have got it made, what is this history of making it, this telling of history? Tall tales, or the telling of tall tales? Telling, or the history of telling? Who can tell, if not you, but who are you to tell such tales? Some shrug their shoulders and go through life mouthing the platitudes that help us get through life. The hard times.

It is what it is.

But who are you to tell? Who can tell.

"A mythology reflects its region," advises the poet of manmade sounds and soundings, and there is no region, as each of us learns, that is without its myths. Either you accept this or you've been thinking too little about who you think you are.

Who *do* you think you are?

And how to make it. And where, in this telling, are we?

And how.

You can like what work does to your body, but not what it does to your soul. And just when you like what it does to your body, your body gives. It lives, it gives. And your soul?

: *They can break you, kid.*

There is no universal man without the particular man. For ain't a man nothin' but a man, feet planted firmly on the ground, water wind and fire turnin' 'round and 'round?

Black white and blue or yellow red and brown, the measure we employ is pound for pound.

~

1958 Rolba System Model R-40, distributed as an American Snowblast machine. 4-speed gearbox, 35 horsepower Volkswagen engine. Throw: 100 feet max. Weight: approximately one ton.

35 *horses*. We take horsepower for granted today, we take fuel for granted, working as so many of us do at such a remove from the mechanisms of mechanical power.

But that's one honkin' machine, don't you know.

From one point of view, there was Joe and Frannie. From another, there was just Joe. From yet another, there was the beginning of something and the end of something. And from any and all points of view, there was work.

~

First week of January 1965, LBJ's "Great Society" speech. In his State of the Union address of the year prior, he'd declared a "War on Poverty." Now, he introduces legislation to provide for all manner of aid—to education, farmers, cities, Appalachia, the poor, the elderly (Administration for Aging), the young (Project Head Start). In March, Operation Rolling Thunder, and John Paul Vann's return to Vietnam. On 7 April, LBJ addresses publicly the "unparalleled brutality" of the war. On Easter Sunday, Writers and Artists Protest runs a large antiwar advertisement in *The New York Times* under the title "End Your Silence." On 30 July, LBJ signs the Social Security Act Amendments, establishing Medicare and Medicaid. On 6 August, he signs the Voting Rights Act; on 3 October, the Immigration and Nationality Act; on 8 November, the Higher Education Act. And on 29 September, the President signs into law the National Foundation on the Arts and the Humanities Act, creating the NEA and the NEH.

Already by the summer, the President is confiding to Lady Bird that he doesn't think the war can be won.

In 1965, Lindsay is elected mayor of New York (William F. Buckley, Jr., one of the contenders), Rocky is still governor, and the first Job Corps camp opens in Maryland. Two Kennedys in the Senate.

In 1965, Pound gives his first public reading in years, in Spoleto. There's a student demonstration in Libya, followed by widespread social unrest and government turmoil. There's a coup in Algeria. UN peacekeeping troops are sent to Cyprus. Podgorny becomes president of the USSR. De Gaulle wins the presidency in France. Malraux meets Mao. There are devastating cyclones in East Pakistan. Streisand wins an Emmy for her TV debut, as does *Sinatra: A Man and his Music*; the networks manage the first public transatlantic telecast; two Gemini spaceships rendezvous in orbit; and HUD becomes a cabinet-level department. The New York World's Fair in Flushing Meadows runs through October, drawing a record crowd at a financial loss. *MAD, Famous Monsters of Filmland, Life, Look, Playboy*. At Berkeley, student demonstrations and a poetry conference. Watts, Guevara, and the same old India-Pakistan-Kashmir conflict.

On the 4th of July, gays and lesbians picket in front of Independence Hall in Philadelphia, the first Annual Reminder.

Two years after the Nuclear Test Ban and *CBS Evening News* expands from fifteen minutes to a half-hour broadcast each night; one year after Nelson Mandela is sentenced to life imprisonment and the debut of Merv Griffin's *Jeopardy* and Leone's The Man With No Name (two years before its US debut) and Marcuse's *One Dimensional Man* and the paperback edition of Friedan's *The Feminine Mystique* and Kubrick's *Dr. Strangelove* and McLuhan's *Understanding Media* and Warhol's *Brillo Box* and Berrigan's *The Sonnets* and Bell's proof of the theorem that bears his name and Monk on the cover of *Time* magazine; the year of Lasch's *The New Radicalism in America* and plate tectonics and Mariner 4 and Nam June Paik's groundbreaking video exhibition. The year before *Flying Saucers, Serious Business* and the founding of the Poetry Project at St. Mark's and Miranda and what upstate New Yorkers will remember as The Blizzard of '66. The year that kids in the US begin bouncing superballs off of anything and everything, and the year that teenagers make the news by taking pep pills and goof balls.

One hundred years after Vice President-elect Andrew Johnson, in an effort to stave off a bout of typhoid fever, makes the mistake of drinking brandy just prior to his inauguration speech. One hundred years after the launch of *The Nation*.

The Sound of Music, Cat Ballou, A Patch of Blue, Doctor Zhivago, The Cincinnati Kid, The Pawnbroker, The Shop on Main Street, The Hallelujah Trail, The Hill, The Sons of Katie Elder, Morituri, Ship of Fools, The Fool Killer, Juliet of the Spirits, Simon of the Desert, Repulsion, Darling, Major Dundee, The Reward, The Ipcress File, The Knack...and How to Get It, In Harm's Way, The Greatest Story Ever Told, When the Boys Meet the Girls, How to Murder Your Wife, The Agony and the Ecstasy, Ride in the Whirlwind, What's New, Pussycat?, Pierrot le Fou, War of the Planets, Othello, The Bedford Incident, Italiani Brava Gente, A Rage to Live, Frankenstein Meets the Space Monster, Boeing Boeing, Battle of the Bulge and *Beach Blanket Bingo.*

Doris Day and Jack Lemmon are hot, Chaplin and Ingmar Bergman are awarded the Erasmus Prize, 007 is still all the rage, and Jerry Lewis kicks off his first telethon for MD.

My Favorite Martian, Daniel Boone, To Tell the Truth, The Ed Sullivan Show, Candid Camera, Lost in Space, McHale's Navy, Combat, The Addams Family, Hogan's Heroes, Gomer Pyle, Green Acres, The Beverly Hillbillies, The Big Valley, Bonanza, Perry Mason, The Man from U.N.C.L.E., Get Smart, The Jackie Gleason Show, Hullabaloo, I Dream of Jeannie, The Wild, Wild West, Petticoat Junction, The Fugitive, The Munsters, The Virginian, Dr. Kildare, Hazel, Andy Griffith, The Lawrence Welk Show, The Smothers Brothers Show, The Jimmy Dean Show, The Andy Williams Show, The Red Skelton Show, The Dean Martin Show, Run for Your Life, Ben Casey, Branded, Shindig, The Lucy Show, Gidget, Ozzie and Harriet, My Three Sons (moves from ABC to CBS), *The Hollywood Palace, The Patty Duke Show, The Dick Van Dyke Show, Gunsmoke, Gilligan's Island, Peyton Place, Bewitched, Honey West, F Troop, Rawhide, Laredo, Flintstones, Flipper, Voyage to the Bottom of the Sea, The F.B.I., Walt Disney's Wonderful World of Color*: a typical week of TV evenings in the US. In the UK, the debut of *Not Only…but Also*. And at year's end, *A Charlie Brown Christmas*. NBC boasts the most programs in color, which probably explains their high ratings.

Playing on Broadway, a three-hour drive from Mannville that not a soul in Mannville takes, are *Fiddler on the Roof, The Odd Couple, Tiny Alice,* and *Flora, the Red Menace*. Brook's RSC production of *Marat/Sade* makes its Broadway debut, and *Hello, Dolly!* is still going strong.

Pop music? How much time you got?

Year of the Snake, among which, Dylan. There's Dylan at Newport and in England, and "like a rolling stone" in July. Queen Elizabeth II awards the Beatles MBEs. The Supremes, the Beach Boys, the Righteous Brothers, the Stones. Canned Heat is formed in L.A. With the addition of Syd Barrett, The Tea Set becomes Pink Floyd. Jefferson Airplane makes its first public appearance in August. The first Fugs album. "Downtown" and "People." It's a five o'clock world. "It's Not Unusual."

Holland/Dozier/Holland. *Getz/Gilberto. The Major Works of John Coltrane.*

Joe and his friends have never heard of Coltrane, or Getz, but they listen around some. They still like The King, and Sinatra, and Chuck Berry, and Buck Owens, and this new guy, Merle Haggard, but they're groovin' to British rock 'n roll too. Wylie's copy of Cosby's *Why Is There Air?* is played, and played, and played, and "Come around idiot, come around" quickly becomes a favorite catchphrase.

Meantime, Tex Ritter is inducted into the Opry, Cash joins The Highwaymen—again—and William Lear develops eight-track audio-tape cartridges. Or was the latter the year prior?

JFK would have turned 48 in May of this year, and babies born in this year will arrive after the baby boom. T. S. Eliot and Winston Churchill and Lorraine Hansberry are gone in January, Malcolm X and Nat King Cole and Felix Frankfurter in February, Chen Cheng and Farouk I and Pepper Martin in March, Edward R. Murrow and Louise Dresser and Linda Darnell in April, Frances Perkins and Sonny Boy Williamson II in May, Judy Holliday and David O. Selznick and Bernard M. Baruch in June, Adlai E. Stevenson II in July, Le Corbusier and Jack Spicer in August, Albert Schweitzer in September, lots of working stiffs in October, lots of working stiffs in November, W. Somerset Maugham in December.

Nearly forgot Nancy Cunard. And Trigger. And Shirley Jackson. So long, farewell, auf wiedersehen, goodnight.

And adios to silver in dimes and quarters.

The standard workweek is estimated at around 39 hours, as compared with 60 hours in 1900. The Bureau of Labor Statistics calculates that the workweek should be down to 32 hours or so by the year 2000. Unemployment is 4.2%. Federal minimum wage is $1.25. Union membership is roughly 17 million, or 24% of employed workers, and roughly one-third of all mothers hold paid jobs. The number of US corporations is on the increase, as is the number of corporate mergers and acquisitions. The population of the US is close to 200 million, with a projected population of 350 million by the year 2000.

Olds introduces the 1966 front-wheel drive Toronado. A new Mustang sells for around $2500. The plastics industry sets a new output record, the electronics industry a new sales record. In October, construction wraps up on St. Louis's Gateway Arch.

The Dodgers win the series in seven against Minnesota. The Celtics beat the Lakers in five. Bill Russell, Oscar Robertson, Jerry West. In the NFL, it's the Packers over the Browns. In the AFL, it's the Bills over the Chargers. Namath signs with the Jets. Sayers wins Rookie of the Year. In hockey, Montreal takes the Stanley Cup. Cassius Clay, now Muhammad Ali, is heavyweight champ, defending against Liston and Patterson, and Stepin Fetchit becomes part of his entourage. Dick Weber wins the men's All-Star bowling tournament, Ann Slattery the women's. Tennis: Australians Roy Emerson and Margaret Smith. Indy and Grand Prix: Jim Clark. Daytona: Fred Lorenzen. Foyt is injured at Riverside, goes on to win other races. In the Kentucky Derby, it's Shoemaker riding Lucky Debonair.

Michigan State takes the national championship in college ball. In college hoops, it's UCLA all the way.

Nobel Prize for Literature: Mikhail Sholokhov. National Book Awards: Norbert Wiener and Theodore Roethke (both awarded posthumously); Saul Bellow; Eleanor Clark; Louis Fischer. The Bollingen: Horace Gregory. Pulitzer (fiction): Shirley Ann Grau. Pulitzer (poetry): John Berryman. Pulitzer (drama): Frank D. Gilroy. Pulitzer (biography): Arthur M. Schlesinger, Jr. Theodore H. White, Edith Sitwell, James Michener, Herman Wouk, Arthur Hailey, Norman Mailer, Katherine Anne Porter, Flannery O'Connor, Nadine Gordimer, W. H. Auden. *Naked Lunch* on trial in Boston. The Prix du Cercle du Livre goes to Georges Cartier, Edouard Glissant returns to Martinique, and Madalyn Murray O'Hair flees to Mexico from Hawai'i via San Francisco. The following year Ken Kesey will fake his suicide and flee there himself to avoid time for drug possession. Carlos Fuentes leaves Mexico for London in 1965 to become a diplomat, while in a public speech in October, Castro reads Che's "Farewell" letter. Here in the States, Gilbert Sorrentino begins his editing stint at Grove Press, while Robert Anton Wilson arrives at *Playboy* as an associate editor.

UNICEF wins the Nobel Peace Prize. In medicine, the Nobel goes to three French scientists from the Pasteur Institute, François Jacob, André Lwoff, and Jacques Monod. In physics, the Nobel goes to a Japanese scientist, Sin-Itiro Tomonaga, and two US scientists, Julian Schwinger and Richard P. Feynman. In chemistry, it's Robert Burns Woodward.

The middle of Marvel's Silver Age: Cap's origin is retold, Spidey fights the Goblin (again), Daredevil leads the Fantastic Four against Dr. Doom, Quicksilver and the Scarlet Witch leave the X-Men, Thor battles Hulk, then "Crusher" Creel, aka the Absorbing Man.

According to Merriam-Webster, *aleatoric* is one of the new words to appear that year. Along with, among others, *anchor man* (broadcasting), *antigravity, antinovel, antiparticle, antipoverty, assemblage* (art), *black box, Black Muslim, biological clock, burnout, commute, electronic music, fail-safe, happening* (performance), *isometrics, kooky, karting, nonbook, pop artist, population explosion, skateboard, split end* (football), *teach-in, torque* (as a verb), *town house,* and *write* (as a transfer of computer data to a storage device). The word *hyper-text* first appears in print in February of 1965 in the Vassar College *Miscellany News,* in an article on a lecture by Theodor Nelson, and east meets west as computers at MIT and System Development Corporation in Santa Monica talk to each other at 1200 bps.

The term *affirmative action* dates to 1965.

Black vernacular words and expressions are gaining popularity: *I mean, like, man, mister Charlie, ofay, cool, dig, hip, you know it, hung up, blood.*

No federally legalized abortion, but abortions. No radar weather forecasts, but weather.

Make the world go away.

~

There's another way to do this, assuming, as I have in the preceding, that my sources are accurate. Sources? Maybe next time, Mack, Mabel.

Here you go:

Two years before the first countertop microwaves, three years before the Big Mac, one year after Don "Monté" Monteverde says goodbye to decal culture, one year after Bowdoin College Museum of Art organizes *The Portrayal of the Negro in American Painting*. The premiere of Balanchine's *Don Quixote*. A second Obie for Sam Shepard. The Beatles at Shea Stadium in August, "In My Life," and the Merry Pranksters among those in attendance at the Beatles's Cow Palace show. Joan Baez's "The New Folk Music" workshop at Esalen. Captain Beefheart joins The Magic Band. The International Poetry Incarnation. Herb Alpert & The Tijuana Brass. Grammies to "Papa's Got a Brand New Bag" and "King of the Road." The Doors. Patrick Sky. Major League Baseball's first amateur draft. Koufax pitches a perfect game, his fourth no-hitter. Chrysler uses Lee Morgan's "The Sidewinder" as background music for a TV commercial during the World Series. *A Study in Terror. Curse of the Fly. Viva Maria! Von Ryan's Express, The Sandpiper, The Spy Who Came in from the Cold, Lord Jim, Genghis Khan, The Flight of the Phoenix, The Battle of Algiers, The Shooting, The Loved One, Love Meetings, The Slender Thread, A High Wind in Jamaica, I Saw What You Did, None But the Brave, Mickey One, Fist in His Pocket, The Satan Bug, Bunny Lake is Missing, Fanatic, The Face of Fu Manchu, The Rounders, Young Cassidy, Young Dillinger, Incubus, Die, Monster, Die!* and *Faster, Pussycat! Kill! Kill!* Warhol's *Vinyl* and *Poor Little Rich Girl*. Doris Wishman's *Bad Girls Go to Hell*. Jones and Noble's animated short, *The Dot and the Line. The Red Balloon?* No, that was '56, not '65. *I Spy*. Wolfe's *The Kandy-Kolored Tangerine-Flake Streamline Baby*. Capote's *In Cold Blood*. Pynchon's *The Crying of Lot 49*. Herbert's *Dune*. Zukofsky. Yurick's *The Warriors*. Markson. Reznikoff's *Testimony*. McClure. Kosinski's first novel. *Stoner*. Matthiessen. *Wild Cat Falling*. Dickey. *Lire le Capital*. Vonnegut. *Seven Love Poems from the Middle Latin*. Salinger's last published work. Metcalf's *Genoa*. Eastlake's *Castle Keep*. Infante's *Three Trapped Tigers*. Aldiss's *Earthworks*. Hunter S. Thompson on Hell's Angels in *The Nation*. Also in *The Nation*, "The Wobbly Spirit," Howard Zinn's review of Joyce L. Kornbluh's *Rebel Voices: An IWW Anthology*. Barthelme's "The Indian Uprising." *Ariel*, posthumously. *The Public Interest*. The reissue of *The Man Who Loved Children. Creepy* the year before, *Eerie* the year after. Rothenberg and Antin's *Some/thing*. LeRoi Jones records "Black Dada Nihilismus" with the New York Art Quartet. Bishop, Ammons, Cormac McCarthy, Valentine, Marguerite Young, Tolson, Trilling, Calvino, Ralph Nader, Haley's X, Snyder, Halberstam, Hofstadter. Arakawa and Gins marry.

Boyd marries Duverger in David Foster Wallace's "Lyndon." *The Milton the Monster Show*. The Moynihan Report. Another year of massive growth in public higher education. On the science and technology front, Robert Dicke's confirmation of the Big Bang, Pioneer 6, COMSAT's Early Bird, DEC's PDP-8, soft contact lenses, Moore's Law, Kevlar, and fuzzy sets. Derinkuyu discovered. Another tome by Herman Kahn. Chevy releases its Mark IV big block. Over 15,000 Datsun 520 pickups sold in the US. The end of Crown Imperial limousines. The M65 field jacket. Chavez leads a nationwide boycott against California grape growers. Peter Jennings's first stint as ABC's anchor. Arthur Treacher joins Merv Griffin. Arlene Croce founds *Ballet Review*. Barbara Rose's "ABC Art." The last Schultz & Dooley commercial. Girard's "imitative desire." Saint Laurent's Piet Mondrian shift dress collection. Aurora's "Bride of Frankenstein" and "Salem Witch" monster models. American Conservatory Theater founded in Pittsburgh, PA. The Chicago Civic Center completed. Viola Liuzzo murdered by the KKK. Ellis Island added to the National Park System. John Harris hanged in South Africa. The second, and worst, Hurricane Betsy. The second, and worst, Palm Sunday tornado outbreak. A fifth of the US wheat crop goes to India, where the monsoon has failed. Evel Knievel's Motorcycle Daredevils. HHH, Jr. Balanchine in *Life*: the ballet "is a woman." Raybert Productions. Max's Kansas City. Hermann Nitsch serves two weeks in prison for his Aktion performances. Rainer's "No Manifesto." Roel van Duyn's Provo manifesto. Brainard's first solo exhibition. Kosuth's *One and Three Chairs*. Damien Hirst is born. Tom Friedman is born. Donald Judd, sounding like Henry James: "A work needs only to be interesting."

OK then? Could be an error or three in there someplace, as I say— check for yourselves, or live with a few discrepancies. Up to you.

Oh & Gatorade is created at the University of Florida.

Isn't that amazing! Especially in retrospect.

~

Childless married men are given the same draft classification as single men. Draft quotas start the year at roughly 17,000 men per month and end the year at 40,000. The maximum penalty for "knowingly" destroying a draft card, a federal offense under a bill signed into law by LBJ, is five years in jail or a fine of $10,000. US troop strength in Vietnam will far surpass the 125,000 mark announced by LBJ in July.

Tell me lies about Vietnam.

March is an especially busy month. The first US ground combat troops—Marines—at Da Nang, the first "walk in space," a ten-minute tour de force by cosmonaut Leonov, and Bloody Sunday—the first "Freedom March" from Selma to Montgomery—followed by Martin Luther King, Jr. leading marchers to the bridge.

By 1965, SDS has 2000 members. In October of 1965, the first public burning of a draft card is staged by the National Coordinating Committee to End the War in Vietnam, another student-run organization.

To protest the war, some—a Catholic man, a Quaker man—are setting themselves on fire.

The sounds of silence.

~

From one point of view, there was Joe and Frannie.

Joe had registered for the draft—he was 1-A, but hadn't given it much thought until the December prior, when his cousin Sammy, in Syracuse, was called up. There was talk that the Navy was planning to draft manpower for the first time in a decade, so Sammy had made a last-ditch effort to enlist in the Navy, hoping to avoid actual combat. No go, and Sammy was now in boot camp—infantry.

Still, Joe's mind was elsewhere. Like most young guys, he didn't really know what to make of the draft, so he chose not to make much of it. And nobody in Mannville seemed too worked up—yet—about Southeast Asia. They knew there was a growing conflict in that part of the world, and some were privately fearful of where it might lead, especially given the escalating nuclear arsenal. But for most of them, and for most of the vets especially, the last world war was the last real war, and Vietnam was, at present, only a distant skirmish. Hell, it wasn't even Korea.

So the local news reported the headlines, but not much else, and most everyone in town figured that "we" were there for good reason, whatever the reason.

What's more, and to the delight of her folks and his mother, Joe and Frannie were talking about getting married. For Frannie's eighteenth birthday, Joe had given her a white gold ring with a tiny Tiffany-set diamond.

If they're not engaged, they sure act a lot like it. They act their age, yes, but as the age demands. And what this age demands of two kids from this economic strata in this part of the world is that they learn quickly, some would say too quickly, how to survive. How to raise and support a family, that tried and true shelter from the storm.

And you see, green-eyed Joe and brown-eyed Frannie have known each other since grade school. When they hold hands, black and white becomes true blue, the color of eternity to those raised under a sky always verging on grey. When they're together, the Sun revolves around the Earth, the stars align themselves in patterns only two pairs of eyes can trace, words become a thicket that this couple and this couple alone can penetrate. The moon smiles a sappy smile when they kiss, TV screens fill with snow, and radio stations broadcast silence while past and future collapse into the present, the present becoming, for an instant, *itself*.

And when they make love for a final time on that clear November eve nine months after the big man first appears at the garage, shooting stars will shuttle across the night sky, a few late season bullfrogs will punctuate the stillness, and the power will go out for hours in the tiny town of Mannville—in fact, the power will go out in all of New York State. The date is 9 November—the Big Blackout.

~

Growing up can be that simple, getting by that elemental. If you've ever found yourself struggling to make ends meet, you know something they don't teach you in school about the land of the free: free you may be, but like everyplace else on the planet, your happiness is up to you, luck or no luck, friends or no friends. And if you've ever felt that core-deep pang of loss that Joe and Frannie will one day feel, you know something they don't teach you in school about the species that wields symbols like tools, and uses tools to make symbols: everybody / loves somebody / sometime.

~

From another point of view, there was Joe.

In this neck of the woods, you learn some hard lessons.

You eat what's on your plate.
You get what you pay for.
You keep to your kind.

Joe has learned the hard way that you keep to your kind. Whenever Joe has put his trust in someone who is not a member of his tight-knit group of friends and family, he's gotten burned. So whether it's transacting a little business or just socializing, Joe treats only a select few in Mannville as actual friends. Everyone else is an acquaintance. The Colellas are family. Wylie and Charlie, friends. Everyone else at the garage, acquaintances. This is safest, and Joe's circle of friends and family is a small circle, one whose members share similar values, similar likes and dislikes.

~

By the time Joe and the big man pull up to the power plant, the snow has started to come down in swirls. The two men have exchanged only a handful of words.

–What's your name?
–Some call me Ant.
–Huh?
–Ant—short for Antonio.
–Oh, Antonio. Yeah. Joe.

Joe takes his right hand off the shift to shake, the big man twisting slightly to the left to return the gesture. He feels the big man's grip wrap entirely around his hand. Big man, big hands. Big, heavily calloused hands.

Joe has never sat this close to a black man—there are *no* black families in Mannville circa 1965—and he has never been alone with a black man. He tries to repress that old saying—big hands, big dick—and he tries even harder to repress that old white anxiety, an anxiety rooted in a mix of racist fears and myths that have somehow been passed along to Joe without his conscious participation. Without thinking, Joe thinks, *black men have bigger dicks.*

Suddenly Joe catches himself thinking this thought, is not sure at first what to do with the thought itself or with the anxiety this thought has produced.

A minute passes.
Another minute.

Slowly a feeling of shame comes over Joe. This big man, he thinks, this man has done nothing to me, so why do I find him such a threat?

So the man is big, so what?
There were bigger men, no doubt, and men smaller than Joe.

So the man is black, so what?
There were blacker men, no doubt, and men lighter than Joe.

So the man has a big dick, so what?
There were men better endowed, as Joe knew from his locker room days, and men not as well endowed as Joe.

What do I care? I'm not sleeping with the guy.

Then Joe remembers the Olds wagon parked in front of the garage, and it dawns on him that this man has a life outside of the pickup, outside of Atlas, outside of shoveling snow, outside of work. Rome apple or no, big hands or no, big dick or no, he's a man, just a man. And Joe recalls then what his old man had told him only months before he died: you judge a man not in terms of how big and tough he is, but in terms of how much he's willing to do for those close to him, how much you can rely on him in a pinch. *A man*, Joe's father said firmly, *must be as good as his word.*

This is how Joe thinks in 1965 at the age of nineteen and having spent his entire life in Mannville, New York.

So Joe decides there and then that he'll not pass judgment on the big man sitting next to him, that he'll give the man a chance to prove himself—the same chance he gives all men. He never stops to consider what the consequences might be of giving the big man the benefit of the doubt. But Joe's mind is made up, consequences or no consequences. This is what makes Joe, Joe.

~

The two men sit quietly together in the cab of the pickup as Joe works all of this out for himself. By the time Joe and the big man pull up to the power plant, the snow has started to come down in swirls. And the white man who steps out of the pickup with the black man is a somewhat different man than the white man who stepped in.

~

From another point of view, there was the beginning of something and the end of something.

Joe and the big man are met by Battaglia's crew, which is led by a rangy guy named DeGroot. DeGroot is a rough and tumble character, but he's what his men call a good guy. Good guys believe in an honest day's work for an honest day's wage.

–Only two?
DeGroot takes off his glove and holds out his hand to shake first Joe's hand and then the big man's, taking note of the big man's large iron shovel.

–This is Ant.
–Pleased as hell to meet ya, Ant.
–Likewise.
–Only two, Joe?
–Yeah, that's how Red called it.
–Red, huh?
–Yeah.
–Well then, that's how Red called it.

Joe and DeGroot smile at each other.

–OK, us three'll take the north end of the spur, you two take the south, and we'll meet up somewhere in the middle.
–Right.
–Raf, Tiny—let's go.

Joe and the big man grab their shovels, swing them over their shoulders, and trudge across a small field toward the south end of the spur, which stops at a massive coal pile. Even with the new accumulations of white stuff, the pile and the area surrounding it is a speckled grey hue owing to the black coal dust beneath, the grey tapering off to white the further north one goes. When they reach the end of the spur, Joe can just make out DeGroot and his crew trudging toward the other end of the spur, a good hundred and fifty yards away. The snow on the tracks is anywhere from two to two-and-a-half feet deep. The only light comes from a row of mercury-vapor lamps strung along the conveyor system sixty yards to the west, alongside the boiler room. It's even darker where DeGroot and his two men have started shoveling.

–Let's get at it. You right-handed?
–Left.

Standing to the left of the big man, Joe swings his shovel off his shoulder and plunges it into the snow, starting at the top layers and swiftly scooping the snow to his left. Within seconds he's at the bottom layer, but as he slams his shovel into it, he's met by more resistance than he's expecting.

–Shit! It's goddamn near frozen!

At nearly the same instant, Joe hears DeGroot shout out something. He can't quite make out what DeGroot is saying, but he can tell from the general tenor that it approximates his own outburst. Joe and DeGroot have a history on such occasions of swapping curses over considerable distances. One problem, Joe realizes immediately, is that he didn't think to bring along a pick, and in any case, using a pick risks damage to the rail ties, so Battaglia isn't likely to have one on hand, either. But how to break through this bottom layer without a pick? It could take all night. And suddenly Joe realizes, too, that he hasn't sensed any motion to the right of him.

He turns to see the big man standing motionless, shovel on his shoulder and staring upward into the sky, the snow falling on his face—in fact, the accumulation of snow is beginning now to obscure his face in a dusting of white. *Like the coal*, Joe thinks, and then catches himself thinking that thought.

–Ant, what the hell are you doing? Let's get to work!

The big man shifts his gaze to Joe in increments, and when their eyes meet, Joe sees something he hasn't reckoned on seeing: *raw fury*. Joe finds himself at once fearful of and mesmerized by the fury in this big man, the fury that this big man has become.

And now it is Joe who is motionless as the big man slowly lifts the iron shovel from his left shoulder with his left hand. He holds it vertically aloft for an instant, as if in tribute to the firmament. And as he lowers the shovel and swings the oak handle to his left side, his right hand comes around in one fluid sequence to grasp the handle perhaps two feet above the iron scoop, and hands and arms and torso align to cock the shovel for its first strike at the snow. In one mighty heave, the iron hits the snow at track level with such impact that the icy bottom layer cracks and splits for five yards down the track, an enormous scoop of white material almost instantly thrown by the big man a good twenty feet to his right. A second strike, and the effect is identical.

He strikes at the snow thus again, and again, and again, and at each strike a muffled impact is followed by a thunderous cracking, the ice and snow hurled to the east side of the tracks, each heave a wheelbarrow of white ice crystals. The big man works with his mouth closed, breathing only through his nose, the only sign that he's exerting himself coming when he snorts as he strikes at the snow with his shovel, and snorts again as he throws the snow to his side.

The big man is waging war against the elements at a rate no man Joe has known can equal. So Joe simply stands in witness as the snow itself seems to tremble in anticipation of each blow, the precipitating substance now granted a life of its own simply by virtue of resisting the big man, nature itself now pitted against what seems to Joe a force of nature.

Or maybe nature has nothing to do with it. Maybe what Joe witnesses, in the aggregate, has no organizing principle beyond the struggle imposed by the social order. By people like and unlike Joe, people who struggle to make sense of their utterances.

In less than one hour and working alone, the big man has cleared nearly one hundred yards of frozen track, while DeGroot and his crew have managed to clear but fifteen yards. As the big man approaches the north end of the spur, DeGroot's crew stops working to stand back, like Joe, and simply watch, not knowing what to make of what they're witnessing. Raf crosses himself as the big man approaches the north end, Joe trailing behind.

–That no ordinary man—that some kind of Juan Enrique.
–Huh?
–You no read about the driving of steel, Tiny?
–Speak English Raf, goddammit.
–When you learn to add, amigo.

DeGroot walks over to Joe.

–What the hell've we got here?
–You tell me.

The big man finishes the spur, stands erect, and leans on his shovel for a few seconds as if to catch his breath. The wind howls up behind him, and the swirls of falling snow, having been displaced by his furious motioning, resume their regular patterns around his stature. Then he turns to Joe, and addresses him in a quiet, relaxed voice.

–Sure could use a cup of hot cocoa and a e-clair right about now.
–Say what?
–I said I sure could use a cup of hot cocoa and a e-clair.

Joe looks at DeGroot, who scratches his head with his gloved forefinger.

–A cup of—hot chocolate?
–Yessir.
–And an eclair.
–Yeah, that's what I said.

Joe can't help but smile, which smile gives way after a few moments, inadvertently, to laughter. A few moments more, and DeGroot begins to laugh, and in less than a minute Joe and DeGroot are both doubled over with laughter, which induces laughter too in DeGroot's men, all four men laughing for all they're worth, their uproar, as it happens, the only human sounds to be heard outdoors for miles around on this dark snowy night in upstate New York in February of 1965.

This goes on for upwards of a minute, during which the big man's expression has changed not an iota.

Not one iota.

—So, how 'bout it?

The big man looks at Joe, who looks at DeGroot.

—What say, DeGroot?

DeGroot shrugs his shoulders.

—Why the hell not? Tell you what in fact—it's on me, hell.

The two crews walk to their respective trucks, Joe and the big man tossing their shovels in the back and Joe brushing off the snow before he gets in. If the big man seems to Joe something more than a man now, he seems at the same time just a man.

For ain't a man nothin' but a man, feet planted firmly on the ground, water wind and fire turnin' 'round and 'round?

Indeed, until we are quite sure that we are not telling one another lies—not being exactly sure who we are—we prefer to tell one another stories which are only nearly true.

Laura Riding, *Progress of Stories*

ACT II

The Wager

5

Oral Culture

–That ain't quite what he said.
–A real he-man, he said.
–Not quite.
–That's what you told me.
–No I didn't.
–What'd he say then?
–He said he'd never seen anything like it.
–Like what?
–Like that much moved that fast.
–So he's a real he-man then, like I say.
–Not quite.
–Well what is it then?
–Something else.
–What?
–The way he said it.
–What d'ya mean?
–I mean, like, he said it like he wasn't sure he believed what he was saying.
–What the fuck's that s'posed t'mean?
–Like as if nobody could do that.
–Nobody?
–Right. Like it couldn't have happened.
–Oh fuck me.

–Well that's how he said it.

–Look, either he did it or he didn't do it. If he did it, it could be done. If he didn't do it, t'fuck we talkin' about?

–He did it.

–If he did it, then it is what it is.

–Then it is what it is, because he did it.

–So I suppose that makes him a real he-man then?

–What if it does, so what?

–So, I don't believe he did it.

–Why not?

–Because, that's why.

–What does that mean?

–Look, for a jungle-bunny to have done that woulda set some kinda fuckin' record.

–How so?

–You ever seen a jungle-bunny that could swim?

–Well—

–No. Just like you never seen a jungle-bunny that could hump it in the cold.

–But—

–So I don't think he did it.

–But he musta done something.

–Sure, so he shoveled some snow faster than those jokers from Battaglia. Faster than your buddy there, what's his name. So they all think he's a real he-man. Am I s'posed to be impressed or sump'in'?

–Well he musta done *something*, Stan. Charlie, what do you think?

–What I think is that I've been busting my butt over here while you two assholes have been arguing the finer points of something about which neither of you knows squat.

–Who says?

–I say. 'Cuz if there's one thing I know, I know that neither of you was there. Now c'mon, give me a hand with these bags.

–OK, OK. Stan, see you at Mickey's later tonight?

–Yeah, but I gotta do a late pick-up over at the warehouse.

–Why the warehouse?

–Fuckers were behind on payments so Baum cut 'em off till they anted up, now the shit's piled so high they're storin' trash inside the buildin'.

–Serves 'em right.

–Yeah. So anyway, I can't make it to the tavern till around eight or so.

–That'll work. Later then.

–Later. And hey, watch yourself with that jungle-bunny, Wylie. You too, she-man.

~

–Too much like work.

–Tell me about it.

–Don't know why in Christ's name they don't bury this stuff. I hear it's been done other places.

–Beats the shit out of me.

–Instead we gotta freeze our nuts off every time grandma hears a little static.

–Yeah. A little wind and cold is all it takes, and that's all we see around here six months of the year.

–Hand me your dykes, will ya Jer. This pair I got here is all but shot.

–Here you go.

–Hear about that new guy over at Atlas, what's his name?

–Ant, I think they call him.

–You guys just about done up there?

–We'll need a few more minutes.

–Jesus Christ but this new guy John is turning out to be a bit of a douchebag, dontcha think?

–Oh yeah.

–So as I was saying before I was so rudely interrupted. Ant, that's it. From Rome.

–Fuckin' those Rome boys. Never know what's up with 'em.

–Hold onto this line, will ya?

–Got it.

–Yeah, so I bumped into ole peep hole with his missus at the Acme the other day, and he's good 'n fuckin' pissed.

–Red's always good 'n fuckin' pissed.

–Yeah, but I never seen peep hole worked up like this.

–What's he so pissed about?

–Well to hear him tell it, this Ant guy is fuckin' up the operation.

–How so?

—Well Red says the other guys think he's a—how'd Red put it?—a "coon Tarzan." Not just some workin' fool, you understand—it's like he's a one-man machine.

—Let me get this straight. Because this guy Ant can work like a dog, or machine, or whatever, Red's pissed?

—That about sums it up.

—That ain't right.

—No, it ain't.

—A man can work, I say leave him be.

—Damn right. Plus the other guys at Atlas look up to this guy Ant, and have taken to giving Red shit when he lays that whip hand on too heavy. Or so says Red.

—I wouldn't mind giving Red some shit. But he's nobody to fuck with.

—And ain't that always the way? You tell a guy like that to blow it out his ass, you risk a new set of teeth.

—Yeah. I wonder how in hell he ended up with that missus of his. She seems like a sweet gal.

—Word has it she's on a *real* short leash. The boss says she's seen marks on her.

—Your wife says that?

—Yeah.

—You know my old man knew Red's old man.

—I didn't know that.

—Yeah. He used to say Red's old man was harder on his wife than on his son.

—C'mon fellas!

—Hold your horses, John. Just another coupla minutes.

—What the fuck with this guy.

—Look good?

—Yeah. Copacetic.

—Copa-who?

—Copacetic. Learned that one in the Jumble this morning.

—You and those Jumbles.

—Yeah, so anyway. So Red acted as if he had something up his sleeve.

—Like what?

—Like who the fuck knows what. But if that miserable bastard has it in for you, he's bound to make your life a living hell, I don't care how much sand is in you.
—Yeah. We done here?
—Yeah. Let me tell douchebag.

—OK John, you can stop watchin' the clock now.

~

—Mind if I ask a question?
—Ask.
—Where'd you learn to work like you do?
—Not sure I understand.
—Yknow—you're a helluva strong guy, and—
—Never been afraid of work.
—Yeah, but—
—Work is work, kid.
—Mind if I ask another question.
—If you got a mind to.
—Why the wagon?
—Good family car.
—You mean, you're married?
—Yeah.
—And you live in Rome?
—Uh-uh—West V'ginia.
—West Virginia? What the fuck brought you to New York then?
—Work. Got a cousin over in Rome.
—So—your wife is back in West Virginia then?
—Yeah.
—What's her name. I mean, if you don't mind my asking?
—Don't mind. Jesse.
—You and Jesse have any kids?
—Not yet.
—We're thinking about kids. I mean, me and my girlfrie—I mean, fiancée.
—Kids?
—Yeah. What's wrong with that?
—Depends.

–Depends on what?

–You.

–Me? I'm outta high school.

–Fresh out.

–I know a few guys my age already settled down with kids.

–No shit.

–What do you mean?

–

–You think I shouldn't get married?

–

–Ant, c'mon.

–What you two—or three, or four—what you gonna do for money?

–Mr. White says I'm due for a raise if I stay another summer.

–How much of a raise?

–Well, a quarter an hour anyway.

–So you be makin'—

–A buck seventy-five.

–So that's, what, maybe four grand a year with overtime?

–Maybe forty-five hundred.

–So that's what you looking at?

–Yeah.

–So that's it then.

–You got any better ideas?

–Gimme a second. Gotta unload this oil drum.

–We usually jockey 'em out on to the edge, then use the loader to get 'em off the truck. Loader's down, Shorty workin' on it.

–Loader's down?

–Yeah, so we wait then. Hey, you don't think you're gonna—

–Stand outta the way.

–What are you————Holy fuck! How the hell'd you pick that thing up? Jesus Christ it must weigh a quarter ton

–

–Ant?

–You were sayin'?

–Je-sus Christ!

–No, 'bout your future.

–Jesus!

–C'mon kid. Ain't got all day here.

–Yeah, well, I was saying—Jesus—I was saying, you got any better ideas?

–You went to high school you said, right?

–Yeah, so?

–Didn't nobody in your school talk about college?

–Yeah, a few of the teachers. My guidance counselor.

–So what'd they say?

–Not much. My old man used to work in the factory, so most of them figured I'd be working there eventually. All but Mr. Loomis.

–This Loomis—what'd he say?

–He said I should think about college.

–So he thought you—whatcha call it? College material?

–He didn't put it quite like that.

–But he said you oughtta be thinkin' on it?

–Yeah.

–Uh-huh. OK then.

–What're you saying?

–Ain't saying nothin'. You doin' all the sayin'.

–I'm supposed to quit my job, leave my girl, go off to college, just like that?

–You tell me.

–I'm supposed to just run off and, what, see the world, is that it?

–Up to you.

–What would you do?

–

–C'mon Ant, what would you do?

–Look, kid: some say it's a small world, some say it's larger than most ever get to see.

–What do you say, Ant?

–

–Ant, what do *you* say?

~

–How's your mother doing?

–Ma is OK. Workin' extra hours at the factory now to make up for the time she lost.

–She up to it?

–It ain't helpin' things any. The operation kinda took it out of her.

–I can imagine. What'd they do, exactly?

–Yknow, I'm still not clear on that myself. My old man calls it women's troubles. But you know my old man.

–How's he doing?

–Same as always.

–Ready for another?

–I can get it—

–No—my round, Wylie.

–OK. Thanks.

–Be back in a sec. Check out that chick over there.

–Way ahead of you.

~

–I'm worried.

–Try not to worry.

–But—

–Listen, try not to worry.

–Aren't you worried?

–Kinda. Yeah, I guess so.

–When will you know?

–There's no way of knowing when exactly. According to the guys down at the VFW, it could come as early as end of the year.

–But not everyone has to go, so why—

–It's luck of the draw.

–I don't believe that.

–Well I don't know what else it is.

–What are we gonna do?

–I don't know. Ant says—

–Ant? That worker you told me about?

–Yeah. He says I should be thinking about college.

–Your friend Ant says that?

–Yeah.

–Well he's right, you know—you should be. Mr. Loomis always said—

–But what about us, our plans?

–Our plans can wait. If it's meant to be, it's meant to be. And if you go to college, you can get out—

–Yeah, maybe. But I mean, what'll the guys think?

–Well, Ant seems to—

—Ant's different.
—Who cares what others think, honey? It's your life.
—What'll your father say?
—I've heard him say he's not even sure we should be there.
—Yeah, but what will he think of me? And anyway, you know what most people will say.
—I don't care what they say.
—But I have a responsibility—
—Your responsibility is to do the best you can to live a happy life, period. And I don't think working at Atlas is the best you can do.
—So what, then? I don't even know how to apply. And what about you?—why aren't you thinking about going?
—I've never been much for studies, you know that.
—But—
—I've got a steady job at my uncle's dealership.
—Working in an office?
—It'll do for now. Maybe someday I'll think about getting a degree in business or something. But right now we need to think about you.
—I don't even know what I'd major in. Business maybe?
—You told me Mr. Loomis wanted you to get a degree in English. My cousin Louisa is a sophomore at Buffalo, and she takes English.
—Like I said to Mr. Loomis, suppose I don't end up as a writer. What the hell can you do with an English degree?
—Well—you can teach.

~

We must work to establish a metric—
you know that's some kind of pentameter?—
in appraising the mood of the weather
say, as a foil for sages with digits.
Not to say that such sages don't get it
right *in imagining it's their inner
life that determines their sense of outer
circumstance?* but there's something more to it
than *cognitive?* causality. What works
inside out *works outside in,* blue collar
a melancholy day? spiteful storm means
a spiteful god? We must be more than clerks

yet clerks too if we would reckon the hard
measure of *habitat* in deeds and dreams.

~

—All's I'm saying, Red, is that I'm spending every other day workin' on
it, is all.
—That's what you're paid to do, ain't it?
—Yeah, maybe. But where's the harm in my making a suggestion?
—Grease monkeys don't get paid to make suggestions.
—Red, listen to reason, will ya? That truck is breakin' down constantly,
and now the tranny is starting to act up. It's had it, Red, and it's holding
up the guys whenever they gotta plow a lot with cars in the way, stalled,
or—
—Lucas, I don't gotta take this guff from a dumb pollock like you.
—I'm not givin' you guff, Red, I'm just tryin' to say—
—I don't gotta take this. Not from you, and not from him, either.
—I ain't heard Ant here say a word, Red. No point in pickin' on him.
—I'll pick on who I pick on. And since when does some third-rate mud
farmer's son think he can tell me how to run my operation?
—No need to make it personal, Red. And I got a right to make a
suggestion, mud farmer's son or no.
—You got no rights unless I say you got rights. Now shut your mouth
and get back to work or take a hike, Lucas.
—But Red—
—I said get back to work or TAKE A FUCKIN' HIKE.

~

—Will you please get off my ass?
—But you don't seem to understand—
—I understand plenty.
—Plenty, but not enough.
—Who made you straw boss of this operation anyway?
—If only you'd stop to consider the impression you're leaving on our
readers.
—I figure that my readers are smart enough to follow what I'm doing.
—Yes, but you have to sell it on the ground.

–And you're saying, what?—that readers don't enjoy reading dialogue? Is that what you're saying?—because my hunch is that they prefer it.

–Dialogue alone cheats the reading experience. We owe our readers more than the vagaries of back-and-forth and inflection. We owe our readers more than mere technique.

–So *you* say. And yet whenever I offer to explain this or that motivation, you jump all over my shit.

–Do you think those are a writer's only options?—dialogue or exposition?

–You're really pissing me off.

–Oh dear. We wouldn't want to do that now, would we.

–Look, let me try one last time to put it in terms you can understand: in her chapter on showing and telling in *Writing Fiction*, Burroway writes— and I quote—that one's "job as a fiction writer is to focus attention not on the words, which are inert, nor on the thoughts these words produce, but through these to felt experience, where the vitality of understanding lies." That's what Burroway says, at least.

–OK, so let's assume that Burroway is correct. We're having a tough time ourselves with the idea that words are "inert," but let's assume she's correct. What you're saying then is that you've focused your attention on "felt experience"?

–Yes.

–Give us an example then.

–An example?

–Yes, a single example. It surely can't be this silly shot-reverse shot exchange of ours. Or better, *simulated* exchange.

–You know what?

–What?

–I'm not gonna give you a fucking example. And you know why?

–Why?

–Because you don't deserve a fucking example.

–But all we're—

–I've tried to be reasonable with you, but you refuse to be reasonable back. And anyway, when it comes right down to it, what it's about is my style, period. And I'll give voice to my style as I damn well please.

–So now everything is to be about "your style" then, and "giving voice" to "your style"? You probably can't even define "voice" and "style."

–Yeah, well—I'm not sure I can define *asshole* either, but I know an *asshole* when I see one.

~

–They say he's only twenty-five.
–Who says?
–Coupla guys down at the Rome shop.
–They gotta be full of shit, no?
–You think so, huh.
–He don't carry himself like that young a guy.
–Maybe not, but there's just no trustin' those darkies, not even when it comes to aging. They see more of life in a year than we do in three. So the young bucks look older, and the old ones don't seem so old 'cause that black varnish don't wanna wrinkle.
–I see what you mean. So why don't you just check your paperwork?
–That's the thing—White keeps it all at Rome.
–So are you saying his number's come up?
–I'm saying it just might have. It just might goddamn well have.
–So how you gonna find out?
–I got friends at the board who're looking into it for me.
–So if it turns out he's on the dodge, you gonna blow him in?
–Sure, eventually. But first we're gonna have some fun with the ape.
–Fun?
–Yeah. I gotta teach these other niggers around here who's boss.
–What's White gonna say?
–White ain't gonna say a goddamn thing. He knows he needs me if he wants this outfit to keep raking in the dough for him.
–Ain't you afraid of what he might do?
–Who, White?
–No, I mean the coon.
–What's that?
–S'posed to be some kinda supercoon or something.
–I ain't afraid of no man.
–But Red, hear tell that he—
–You just remember that, Buster—*no man.*

6

Tenpin

The second crew consists of Mr. White's two nephews, his sister's sons Billy and Nicky, both high-school dropouts and highly unreliable as far as putting shoulder to wheel; and Dean, a wiry man of sixty-five and a third-generation dairy farmer who's seen better days, but who, as they say in this neck of the woods, knows how to work.

Dean is a story in himself, a man who, by the time he was twenty, had learned all of life's important lessons, save one: *nobody knows you when you're down and out.* He'd learned this last lesson the hard way, when his farm was going under.

Dean's crew sees much less action than the first crew, and is called in once or twice a week and on an emergency basis. Once in a great while the two crews overlap.

Red treats both crews about the same, but has more contempt for the men of the first crew simply because they're more productive. Which is to say, the second crew lives up to Red's generally low regard, and this pleases Red. This does not please Dean, however, who has on occasion complained to Red about the nephews. Red has in turn instructed Dean each time to "make the most" of the situation, "or else."

Red's "or else" is translated by Dean, as by everyone else on the payroll at Atlas, to mean that Mr. White will intervene and, as Shorty puts it, "heads will roll." In truth, Mr. White would probably let Dean go before firing his sister's sons, but Red has no intention, in any case, of informing on them. And Dean's work ethic is such that he would likely find it incomprehensible were he to learn that Red actually enjoys seeing his mules at odds with one another, and seeing his boss's nephews cheat their loaded Uncle Marty.

It's been two weeks to the day since the big man first set foot in the garage, and everyone at Atlas is already aware of the growing tension between Red and Ant. Red refuses to address the big man directly, assigning work orders to others and referring to Ant only in the third person. At the same time, the fact that Ant has evidently taken Joe, and to a lesser extent Wylie and Charlie, under his wing clearly does not please Red.

~

Editor feels obliged to comment briefly upon the rather extraordinary liberties taken in the last chapter by our M. Wylie. Doubtless it will seem to most readers that M. Wylie has dutifully exempted himself from any charge of authorial intrusion, save for that one curious tête-à-tête (which may well have been intended as a mockery of our concerns). Nevertheless, careful readers will be sure to note that the (generally well executed) dialogues are, at their best and in the strict sense, works not of the imagination, but to employ Coleridge's happy distinction, products of sheer fancy (we know, for instance, that real people do not talk this way). For all of their entertainment value, they exhibit little if any lasting truth-value, compromised as they are by M. Wylie's wholesale departure from the precincts of narration. Literature, to be literature, is description first, demonstration second (together these constitute *showing*), explanation last (*telling*). When M. Wylie isn't busy explaining himself, he seems to believe that demonstration is a substitute for description, that to show is but to *display*.

The man has forgotten himself.

Such vulgar realism was touched on long ago by M. Frye when he suggested that the "literature of experience" (his umbrella term for realist modes) approached a "representative likeness to life" that mythological modes eschewed in favor of more "abstract and conventionalized" structures (*Anatomy of Criticism*). Such a "likeness to life," we would observe, has led some (most?) readers to conceive of the literary strictly in terms of representation, a longstanding habit that continues to haunt the production and consumption—to employ the unreconstructed binary—of unconventional, nonrepresentational artifacts.

Irony and satire, then, much as other "low mimetic" modes, dwell in such realisms because the hero of such tales is "one of us." Of the characters in the story unfolding before us, in fits and starts, Joe would be a protagonist of sorts, and he is "one of us." He is our chief point of contact with the strongman other—the big man.

But what of the big man? Is he a "high mimetic" hero—"a leader," in M. Frye's succinct terms, something of a *primus inter pares*; or is he more properly a romantic hero, the doer of great deeds, the folk hero, the living legend (for M. Frye, the register as well of allegory); or is he perhaps a "divine being," the stuff of myth? Under our intrepid anatomist's categorizing gaze, all plot types or morphologies (see M. Bettelheim, M. Propp, M. Lotman's semiotic, Jung, etc.) can be grouped according to four *mythoi*, or "generic plots," and each generic template corresponds to a heroic figure. (Similarly, in M. Calvino's treatment, myth is the repetitive groundwork for "fables," by which he means plots ["Myth in the Narrative"].) Of the four mythoi—romance, tragedy, comedy and irony—irony (satire becoming "militant irony") is for M. Frye best understood as a "parody of romance," its seasonal datum being the "mythos of winter." For heroes who are like us, we may locate the analog to their mortal failings in the natural world's perennial and partial death.

But can we really speak of the tale at hand as a "parody of romance"? An additional complication is M. Frye's admission that the five fictional modes (myth, romance, high and low mimetic, and ironic) "evidently go around in a circle," with the mythoi themselves blending "the ideal and the actual" to yield romantic tragedy, comic romance, and so forth.

The blurring of modes and mythoi signals a chief liability of applying structural principles *ex post facto* to a broad range of human (symbolic) endeavor, and then treating the critical result as identifying the generative conditions of the creative act (which is not to deny the utility of such interpretive tactics).

Further, as M. White has observed, M. Frye's categorical approach to genre may in fact overstate the degree of separation thereby posited between "discursive writing"—writing with an explicit *dianoia*, or theme, such as historical writing—and fiction or poetry (*Tropics of Discourse*). Anything not belonging clearly to either domain becomes, given M. Frye's schema and as M. White elaborates, a "bastard genre," and the idea that events might be narrated in accordance with a principle of selection that configures them not in accordance with their intrinsic value but with attention to whether they simply and profoundly *fit* in the intended storyline (a process M. White calls "emplotment") is lost on our Quebecois ordained minister (and if M. White is correct, lost on M. Collingwood, as well).

To be sure, M. Frye would grant that, ultimately, the *formal* differences between history and, say, poetry comprise the only substantive distinction in play, for all discursive writing enacts, at some level, the structural solicitations of myth; thus, setting aside a lurking formalism that would grossly understate reception realities, the distinction, for M. Frye, between history and poetry becomes a matter of formal degree and variation. This is quite apart from M. Cassirer's having advanced the "mythic mode" of language—the archaic word, the word endowed with "physico-magico power"—as "the first form in which the spiritual power inherent in language can be apprehended at all..." (*Language and Myth*).

As to the "*stolen* mythic power" Mme. Daly has located in "patriarchal myths" (*Gyn/Ecology*), we, M. Wylie *and* myself, can only hope to have mitigated the effects of same. You be the judge.

We have some recollection, too, of M. Kermode having commented on the distinction between myth and fiction (in which regard he would valorize fiction, as we recall—see *The Sense of an Ending*); and we have of course neglected the work of so many others, and in particular, the substantial body of inquiry by M. Lévi-Strauss, whose discussion of the "mytheme," a term he aligns with M. Jakobson's conception of the phoneme, may be apposite to our discussion here (*The View from Afar*). For another time, perhaps.

At any rate, as we have been at some pains to communicate to M. Wylie, there is an articulatory consistency, a self-presence of form, to which all authors must attend, even when negotiating the morass of contemporary formal devices and critical-theoretical logics and postmodern bogeymen. (In our more peevish moments, we would want our author to detail, for instance, the implied relationship between his imagined speech patterns, as putatively transcribed in his last turn, and something akin to M. Ong's "voicings" [*Orality and Literacy*].) One may abrogate narrational responsibility only when certain qualifications obtain in its wake, and M. Wylie, by opting to provide us with raw dialogue, would leave us only with native conjecture—our individual lights, conditioned as they may be by our cultural circumstances—as a tool by which we may pry open the reality of his mythology, or romance, or fiction.

Without wishing to state the matter too forcefully, then, we far prefer M. Nelson's recent excursion into the pertinent lore. That is, we far prefer the nonfictional as an implement for pursuing, if ultimately undoing, the mythical. In the terms M. Eco sets forth in 1972, such undoing is a matter of permitting the mythical character to "consume himself"—to become, in the course of events, mortal. Rather like the myth of Hercules, as presented for instance in Mme. Hamilton's classic treatment.

The prior paragraph's caveat aside, M. Whitehead's stimulating romp circa 2001 through mythic territory, to which that limned herein bears a marked resemblance, ought at least to incline readers to reflect on all corresponding adumbrations.

Continuing, then, with our exposition:

~

Football, baseball, basketball, billiards, bowling.

Bowling.

On Tuesday nights, weather permitting—which is to say, when the weather is not such as to require the application of perspiring Atlas bodies to accumulations from the sky—Joe, Wylie, Charlie and Dean can be found after six p.m. at Bob's Alley Cats, for league play. Dean, the anchor, is a scratch bowler, Charlie and Wylie are so-so (Charlie sometimes brings along her daughter Sally, and is usually distracted as a result), and Joe rolls a respectable 180 average. As the Atlas Titans, the four have developed a reputation for being at once unreliable—owing, again, to the weather, which has forced three forfeits already this season—and tough to beat.

A sizable quantity of Carling Black Label is consumed on these occasions, and of the four, Dean is known for imbibing heavily with minimal negative consequences for his game. Shorty sometimes drops in to chat with his fellow workers and "lend a little moral support," as he puts it—and also to have a beer or two with the guys.

Red keeps away from these affairs as a rule, but on this particular Tuesday night he's seated in the bar area, huddled over a beer with Buster, his back to the lanes. The team members eye the two suspiciously.

Wylie has been having a hard go of it on the lanes this evening, having pulled the nail half off on the middle finger of his left hand in a work mishap. After missing a 1-2-4 spare, he walks over to the front desk to see if he can scrounge up a Band-Aid. Dean stands to pick up his ball as Baum's Haulers' anchorman, Stan, returns from the line on the lane adjacent, shaking his head at having picked up only three pins on his first roll. The Haulers are down by some forty pins. Dean winks at Joe, coughing out in a low growl, "Keep your eye on the two buzzards."

Just as Dean says this, Buster rises and walks over, Red still with his back to the action. As Buster approaches he's stopped by Mac, also on the Haulers. Mac wants to ask Buster something about his new gas range, but Buster brushes him off with a "give me a call later" and a pat on the back. Buster walks into the lane area all smiles and handshakes, and seats himself where Dean had been sitting, between Joe and Charlie, who tonight is without child. Like Joe, Charlie nurses a beer. On these occasions Charlie unknots her long brown hair and lets it fall around her shoulders in an attractive tangle. Appearances to the contrary, this has no effect whatever on her temperament.

"So, kissed any ass we should know about?" is Charlie's opening salvo. Buster is—how to say this?—flustered. Things go downhill, approximately, from here, and it would be uncharitable to report in graphic and complete detail Charlie's obscene repartee, her ruthlessly ingenious, rapid-fire assault not simply on Buster's character, but on his very mode of being, to which the poor sod can in response garble only a syllable or two. (Buster is balding, flabby, has bad teeth and poor hygiene, wears thick horn-rimmed glasses, dresses sloppily, has made it through the eleventh grade and picks his ears constantly. He's got a way with pumps and motors, his sole source of self-esteem.) By the time Dean has rejoined his team members—an easy if disappointing spare to follow his four consecutive strikes—Joe is on the verge both of incontinence and of feeling sorry for Buster, and Charlie is in the midst of remarking on Buster's unclipped nose hairs, advising that he should attend to same because "they're a telltale sign of whose butt you're brownnosing—same stink. And you know what they say—the stink marks the fink."

Dean interrupts, sensing that Buster has been sent by Red not to spy on the four, but with an agenda. He manages to restore Buster to some measure of composure by small-talking him down from Charlie's accelerating barrage. Once Buster has his wits about him, Dean asks, with all the innocence his world-weary eyes can muster, "What's up?" And Buster proceeds to lay Red's little wager before Dean, Joe, Charlie, and Wylie, who's back at the lanes with a bandaged finger.

~

We might do well to observe at this point that, to whatever degree mythology *is* at stake in these proceedings, M. de Man's remarks on foundational (structural) myth provide apt caution here. For if, as M. de Man argues, the "unity of traditional myths" requires " a privileged point of view to which the method itself denies any status of authenticity"—that is, a point of view that wants not to be taken *as* a point of view, but as a given—the matter becomes even more perplexing when the denial "involves the disappearance of the self as a constitutive subject" (*Blindness and Insight*).

To the extent, then, that we are flirting with "traditional myths," we must be careful not to permit our point(s) of view to operate without adequate illumination—indeed, we must question the conditions of the authentic as such (as in some sense we are busy doing, *here*). And yet we must balance this requirement, we feel, against our stated desire to avoid an excess of reflexive flotsam. For the record, note that no one has advocated "the disappearance of the self as a constitutive subject," whether these (discrete?) subjects are narrational (M. Wylie, ourselves, etc.), authorial (M. A_____, for one), or characterological (M. Wylie again, Joe, the big man, etc.). And while it is true that our status, as Editor-narrator, *tends* in that (omniscient) direction—third person narration may in general be something of a disappearing act, to varying degrees—we would never deny our constitutive positioning; our mode of telling clearly inflects all that falls under its presumed purview. Still, all self-styled authorial selves must get out of the way occasionally if only to let things *happen*.

Additionally, as Mssrs. Deleuze and Guattari (building on M. Duvignaud's writings) speculate in a more anthropological light, there may be other "phenomena pervading societies that are not degradations of the mythic order but irreducible dynamisms drawing lines of flight and implying other forms of expression than those of myth," ultimately to be recuperated by myth "in order to curb them" (*A Thousand Plateaus*).

Viewed in such terms, the mythic mode obscures as much as it reveals, which would seem to jibe with Mme. Langer's observation that "in tribal societies there is frequently no real body of myth, no coherent dogma at all, and contradiction does not trouble people" (*Mind: An Essay on Human Feeling*, v. III). "They seem," Mme. Langer reports of members of such societies, "to think of a single narrative at a time, as one does with a fictitious story, but while they tell it or contemplate it thus in isolation they believe it."

Mme. Langer's commentary may suggest an alternative, then, to the formal self-presence we advocate above, and her ensuing remarks regarding the motivation for myth ("Ritual is almost certainly older than narrative") imply that there may be more primal, if not primitive (by which we do not thereby mean impoverished), elements at work in the tale before us. But we will preserve our (creolized?) narrative position here, as it seems the prudent, if not expedient, answer to the present (circa 2011, app-based) world of positional, if not relational, possibilities, and far preferable to permitting the pretense of everyday speech to plump for one's passions. For that matter, if the desired effect is imagined as having less to do with verisimilitude than with facticity, research has shown (please trust us on this) that neither purely fictional accounts nor unalloyed presentations of urban legend and the like will fare as well in convincing readers as will hybrids of the two, or mutations of the two, or...

Continuing, then, with our exposition:

~

At the same moment that Buster is taking bets at the alley, Ant is pulling up to his cousin Elvin's rundown two-flat in Rome. He turns his wagon into the long, frozen-over gravel driveway and parks alongside a beat-up metallic green Impala, the Impala parked half inside of the ramshackle garage structure, its hood up. Ant steps out into the clear, cold night—it's a quiet evening in the neighborhood—and he glances skyward, pausing for a few seconds to take in the star-spangled ceiling. He walks to the entrance at the rear of the house, and just as he inserts the key to unlock the door to his small, unfinished bedroom, he hears his cousin calling him from the front porch. About all he can make out is "Mr. Oldsmobile."

He walks around front. Elvin evidently wants Mr. Oldsmobile to go easy on the small space heater that Ant has in his bedroom—his only source of heat. Ant nods. Elvin informs Mr. Oldsmobile that, "cousin or no cousin," he won't have any "freeloaders" running up his electric bill, especially not now that Elvin's wife Etta is expecting. Mr. Oldsmobile informs Elvin, in a quiet voice, that his next paycheck is due in a few days, on receipt of which he will amply reimburse Elvin for his generosity, as he has right along. Elvin is still not satisfied, and accuses Mr. Oldsmobile of running up his electric bill "on account of that no-good fish bowl" which Elvin has "a mind to flush down the toilet." At which last Mr. Oldsmobile makes a slight motion toward Elvin, but checks himself. Which gesture cools Elvin down considerably, his wife Etta calling him back into the house even as he leaves Mr. Oldsmobile with a hastily uttered "don't matter to me *who* yo mama be."

Ant walks around back, unlocks the door to his bedroom, and steps inside. Elvin's allegation notwithstanding, the room is dark and cold, and Ant reaches to his left to turn on a lamp, which sits atop a small pine dresser next to the now infamous fish bowl, inside of which shimmers a solitary goldfish. Ant tests the temperature of the water by gently dipping the tip of his large forefinger in the bowl, the goldfish swimming up to greet his finger. Then he bends down to turn on the small space heater. As the machine whirs away, Ant opens the top drawer of his dresser, and takes out a small canister of fish food, sprinkling a tiny portion on the water's surface. The goldfish swims up to nibble on the food specks, Ant muttering under his breath, "Go get 'em little man."

7

Backstory

To those who had known him in the early fifties, when he still aspired to a university appointment, Augie Loomis was a lapsed modernist, someone for whom the repressive realities of McCarthyism, Eisenhower-era quietism and populist anti-intellectualism demanded a more efficacious artistic response than might be had by "tinkering with form," as he would come to call it. To use a language unavailable to Dr. Loomis at the time, but embodying something of his attitude toward the times:

> The relation between art and life has become so strained, uncertain and problematical that ever more artists have, in their work, dared the flight into a sphere that is no longer that of life as it is actually lived and no longer shows or even demands a recognizable connection with the "concreteness" of human existence. Shunning the ever more difficult alliance with the "real," art has been tempted to settle where it is at last left to itself: in the domain of abstraction and pure form. (Erich Heller, "Autobiography and Literature")

Of course this latter would constitute, for some, an entirely too pessimistic appraisal of a key development in the arts. A scant eight years after Heller's summary dismissal (which he had offered by way of praising Thomas Mann), Raymond Federman could enthusiastically describe this development, all told, as the salient answer to the provocations of Artaud, Sartre, Robbe-Grillet and so many others:

> Modern Art and New Fiction reveal that we exist in a temporary situation, surrounded by temporary landscapes. Faced with this transitory aspect of life and of the world, literature confronts its own impossibility.... It searches, within itself, for its subject, because the subject is no longer outside the work of art, it is no longer simply Nature or Man. ("Fiction Today or the Pursuit of Non-Knowledge")

To paraphrase Federman: some viewed as auspicious the emergence of a literature that, for instance, sought to catalog what exists *in* the world and how it exists, as opposed to what we (think we) know *of* the world. Radical skepticism as to literature's erstwhile metaphysical claims thus produced an empirical surplus, limited only by the seemingly boundless limits of form.

~

Such were the opposing aesthetic rationales, at any rate, often presented in their incipient stages, that greeted Dr. Loomis in the pages of the many arts journals and newspapers of which he had made it his business to keep abreast. Yet owing in the final analysis as much to the temperament of our good doctor as to his generational circumstances, an aporia of sorts eventually took root in the man's apprehension of his place in the sun.

~

Having witnessed his students growing up absurd, as it were, while progressively catered to, first in dribbles and spurts and later in deluge, by the likes of the New Left and the Free Speech Movement and the Feminine Mystique and TV and rock 'n roll and sexual liberation; and having himself admirably refused, much like his contemporary Irving Howe (whom he had once had the pleasure of hearing give a lecture), to renege outright, in the name of some newer, ostensibly more "radical" politics, on his fealty to those venerable, homegrown traditions of collective political engagement, whether more socialist or more liberal in character, that had emphasized bread and butter issues; the securely middle-class if uncomfortably middle-aged Dr. Loomis had found himself gradually occupying a personal-political orbit at some remove from what, to his way of thinking, were the frenzied revolutions of the present, and in particular, at some remove from the vigorously antiestablishment, anti-corporate devotions of that small cadre of iconoclastic seniors that surfaced each and every term at Mannville High, which cadre was, to Dr. Loomis's dismay, growing with each successive term more and more alien to him.

He had, again, resolved to forgo his years of fascination with the arts of juxtaposition, collage, fragmentation and the like to endorse instead an artistic orientation that, in his view and in the view of like-minded others, addressed with more urgency the question of social relevance in the arts. To state the matter concisely: Dr. Loomis had abandoned radical modernism and its discontents to become a student and an acolyte of the Beat Generation—which, if modernist, was yet to his way of thinking something else again, given its vatic preoccupations. He had subsequently left the quadrangle not as a failed scholar, but as a teacher—he insisted on "Mr. Loomis" as much to encourage informal reception by others as to allay any residual professorial pretense he might himself harbor—and his hope was simply to work as much good in the classroom as one might muster. Indeed, until recently he had served, by any measure, as a humane, dedicated, and inspiring mentor to each new crop of Mannville's teenagers. And as if in tribute to his former scholastic trappings, in which he had even in his short tenure begun to develop a reputation as an incisive commentator on the state of the arts, Mr. Loomis championed the Beats to such an extent that his efforts to promote their work and mindset had occasionally earned him the intense scrutiny of Mannville High's administrators, a scrutiny he wore much as a badge of honor.

But as the sixties unfolded, and in spite of those cultural niches in which a Kerouac or a Ginsberg or a di Prima would always be held in high esteem, Mr. Loomis's passion for the Beats and their rhetoric availed him less and less when it came to *relating*—a word his students

were then learning to use to denote a prevailing simpatico—to his daily
milieu. Had he been a Beat through and through, had he really
understood the growing potential of *media* as such to shape the social
domain, it is possible that our Mr. Loomis might have prevailed with
his students, and in ensuing years, might have helped to guide their
desire for more direct political action and lasting social change. But
having one foot planted solidly in the yesteryear of the avant-garde,
with its crop of politically inept avant-gardists—not all of them, of
course, but a fair number—proved fatal to his capacity to appreciate
fully, for instance, the positive correlation between booming electric
guitar riffs and social rebellion. The student body at Mannville was
slowly but surely tapping into a subterranean movement that would, as
Mr. Loomis had correctly intuited, position the Beats as but a phase,
albeit a strategic phase, in the general and fraught upheaval of postwar
social mores. And neither our bachelor's estimable intelligence nor his
teacher-to-student bonhomie could offset the encroaching grey
envelope that loomed on his horizon, less colorfully realized in his less
bardic moments as the inexorably mundane discourse of *retirement*. Mr.
Loomis was becoming, day by day, *useless*, and had he been a child of
some later pedagogical era, he might have been able to turn his growing
uselessness to some decentered advantage, or at least, to chalk it up to
circumstances beyond his control. But as a creature of an age steeped
in social utility and can-do conformity, and a creature no less that had
rebelled *against* his age, his psychosocial make-up was somewhat more
fallible.

In all, one might say of Mr. Loomis that he had missed the boat; that
the train had left the station; that the parade had passed him by; that
the sun had risen and set on his aspirations; that he could no longer
properly be called a—look out—*kid*. And in a desperate attempt to
prove his mettle and get with the times, Mr. Loomis faltered, falling
entirely out of character.

He began to drop acid.

~

Now, had Mr. Loomis recourse to anything like a support group—he
would not have had access to the term itself until the end of the

decade—a little Lucy might not have been such a bad thing. But sitting alone in his bookshelved, beanbagged, bedraggled, bohemian-style living room two or three nights a week with the lights turned down low and with "Norwegian Wood" playing over (and over) on his phonograph—he had, years prior, taken a (highly flammable in fact) flat above the Victory Market on Main Street—the most popular teacher at Mannville High from 1957-1963 entered a private psychedelic realm whose aftereffects were such that his professional profile and responsibilities seemed to him, hit by hit, but a distant, inconsequential pursuit. And as a result, even his most loyal students were beginning to grow impatient with this eccentric man whose ever more frequent episodes of absentmindedness and oblique, if erudite, wit were marking him with each passing day as an eccentric failure. To the young, country-bred, but increasingly hip scholars of Mannville, New York, Mr. Loomis was, on or off the job, just a little out of it.

To all but Joe—Joseph—Amato, that is, for whom Mr. Loomis represented the sole lifeline to the world of lifeways leading away from Mannville. Joseph, fatherless at this crucial age, had all the reason in the world to respect a man of such failings, noble failings to those few town residents who could get past the rumor that Mr. Loomis was an "addict" (nobody had access to "druggie" in 1965, else it might have been the preferred, and more accurate, term). Mrs. Amato was, happily for Joseph, one of those faithful few, for she had known Mr. Loomis socially for some years, as had her late husband, and she knew in her heart of hearts that he was a good man, intent on doing only good for her only child.

~

So when Mr. Loomis asked Joseph to meet with him after school one mild December afternoon six months prior to graduation to "assess" the young man's "situation," the seventeen-year-old, while on the one hand enthusiastically predisposed toward Mr. Loomis's generous offer of assistance, was nevertheless overcome by the same feelings of ambivalence most working-class young adults of mid-sixties America experienced when change was at hand, when the possibility of profound gain was matched by the probability of profound loss. Yes, he wanted out, yes, he wanted to make something of himself, but no, he did not want to leave the security of home, of Mom, of Frannie, of a good day's wage for a good day's work. And at ten a.m. on the Thursday he was to meet with Mr. Loomis, while jogging across the runoff trickling from mounds of melting snow, an early thaw—Mr. Travis, the gym coach, insisted on having his athletes lap the parking lot at the end of each class period, "snow or no snow"—Joseph wondered what the future held in store for him, and wondered whether his striding escorts were wondering the same thing.

~

–Hello, young man.
–Hi, Mr. Loomis.
–Have a seat.

Mr. Loomis's office was stuffed with overstuffed metal bookshelves. An Underwood typewriter sat on a small stand next to his desk, and next to this stand was a large metal filing cabinet. The blinds were drawn, and the warm glow of a single desk lamp helped to offset the institutional sterility of steel desk and vinyl flooring and yellowed paint. There was an odd and oddly familiar smell in the office that Joseph would later identify, to his puzzlement, as clove. He could not know that Mr. Loomis had grown fond of burning the incense at home, and that the scent now permeated not only his clothing, but his person.

–I've asked you here because I believe it's high time we discussed your plans.
–I don't really have any plans, Mr. Loomis, other than to find work.
–I see. And may I ask, what does Rose—your mother say about this? How *is* your mother, anyway? I haven't seen her in quite a spell.
–She's doing fine. I haven't really talked to her about it. I think she'd be happy just to see me graduate.
–You'll graduate, Mr. Amato, not to worry. Can we talk for a moment about your writing?
–Sure.

Mr. Loomis picked up a stack of papers on his desk, resting the stack on his lap and thumbing through as he spoke.

—Well you see, when I read your last piece, where I had you attempt to mimic the style of—
—I enjoyed writing that.
—Yes, I could tell. You—ah, here it is. Yes, you've done an excellent job here matching the shifts in narration. Tell me—do you do a lot of reading at home?
—You mean, what you assign?
—No—well yes, but no. I mean, on your own. Do you like to read?
—Well my mother—and father—they always said it's important to read. So when I was a kid they were always buying me a book for my birthday, Christmas, you know. I read a lot of classics.
—Classics?
—You know—H. G. Wells, Jules Verne, Mark Twain.
—I see, I see.

Mr. Loomis rocked back in his swivel chair, eyes squinting at his belly, and as he was wont to of late, lost himself in thought. Or so it seemed to Joseph, who felt not a little awkward as Mr. Loomis's self-absorption approached the two-minute mark.

—Mr. Loomis?
—
—Mr. Loomis?
—
—Mr.—

Mr. Loomis bolted upright in his chair.

—Love and honor and pity and pride and compassion and SACRIFICE!

Joseph was dumbfounded, his startled expression bringing Mr. Loomis to.

—Never mind, nothing, nothing. Just thinking aloud, something, something from. Long ago. Nothing. Listen, my young sir: you belong in college.
—But—
—But nothing. You belong in college.

–But my mother, we have bills to pay, Mr. Loomis. Besides, I don't know how to apply, and—

–Where there's a will, Mr. Amato.

–Mr. Loomis, you have to understand—it's not that I don't appreciate your help, but—

–I'll tell you what I'm going to do. Our little academy here in the wild doesn't really have the resources to conduct a thorough search—and I'm not—my memory isn't quite what it used to be, back when I, when I knew—

Mr. Loomis smiled to himself at this last, and again drifted off into a private reverie, and Joseph felt for his instructor. Sure he was pushy, but he was genuine, and even at seventeen, Joseph knew you couldn't put a price tag on that.

But as the seconds became minutes, Joseph came to feel something more than compassion for the man seated before him. Without even being aware of it, Joseph was learning the final lesson that Mr. Loomis would teach him, and it was a lesson taught inadvertently: that humility ought to have nothing whatever to do with indigence.

–Mr. Loomis?

–Yes?

–You were saying that—we don't have the resources—

–Yes, of course, resources, right. So. I'm going to get in touch with a dear friend of mine, a reference librarian at _____ downstate. And I'm going to ask her if she might help us to compile a list of schools where you might make application—good schools, with good English programs, and schools that won't cost you an arm and a leg in tuition. How's that sound?

–Sounds good, I guess. I'm a little concerned about—my mother and I don't have a lot of—

–Just for starters, Mr. Amato. First we compile the data, then we decide what we can do with what we have. OK?

–OK. But Mr. Loomis, what am I going to do with—an English degree? I mean, I like English and all, but—

–It's the best preparation for a writer, Mr. Amato. A *writer*, which you have the talent for, lad, if not the stomach. Time will tell, and in any case, writers need to know how to *read*.

–Mr. Loomis––
–Yes lad?
–Just wanted to say that––I really appreciate everything you're doing for me, Mr. Loomis. Means more to me than I can say.
–No need to say anything, lad, no need to say anything.

And with that, Mr. Loomis abruptly ushered Joseph out of his office, and immediately set about composing a letter to his confederate and fellow Beat aficionado, Imogene Perkins.

And later that evening, the galaxies would descend with the darkness upon Augie Loomis's living room, and amid the nebular swirl of stardust and heavenly bodies and serotonin receptors, he would mysteriously and accurately and with exceptional clarity foresee that, like so many others whose lives were to be cut short by bad choices or bad circumstances or bad luck, or all three, he would not live out the decade.

8

Revelations

Praiseworthy, the work of laborers, the work of men and women who work like machines.

Praiseworthy, the work of names, the work of signing and singing, the work with or without letters.

"It's who I am."
"It's not who I am."

Wage earners find it impossible to avoid the grammar of ontology.

To mythify, to demythify. It's so twentieth-century. And better than wages?

"A mythology ravels and unravels. It is a knowledge, a science of life open only to those who have no training in it. It is a living science which begets itself and makes away with itself."

Did Aragon have in mind what we with secular ambitions have in mind?

"It would seem that we are condemned for some time yet always to speak *excessively* about reality."

Did Barthes have in mind what we with secular ambitions have in mind?

"Vote for me."

And what about Freud's "wish-phantasies" of the nation-state?

"Yes, it's us."
"No, it's not."

Etc.

Do I resist myself? Very well then, I resist myself.

"A poem with history," recall. "Make it new."
Make *what* new?

"When men were men and women were men and boys were girls."

The key, you will note, is to avoid being a boy or a girl, because these are to be distinguished from the men. As are ladies and gentlemen, ladies and gentlemen.

Man, it's comforting to think this way once in a while. Isn't it?

Bring it down to ground level, you think you got it made, stranger. Especially if your theory appears to have no history, and your history no theory. And if neither would provide evidence of class warfare. Just fabulous.

Corporations (which have a history) absorb. Anything, everything, even the Blob, he says, poker-faced. (McQueen was big then too, in a saddle, on a Harley, at the card table.)

Permit me to be not avant-garde, but simply next
in line, and we will try to do something not new, but a

new. Important? Too much so to decode, as in,
poeticize.

Or, could be. Remember: forget it: the image. Unless or until you're a Man With A Movie Camera. That is, storied. In man-hours.

"Even if I could write like that, I wouldn't."

More voiceover.

"I'm just giving you the treatment."

Uh-huh, exactly so. And really, laughter may be the best way to get on, or get off. You just have no idea.

"I have no one particular in mind."

Everyone then? To motion beyond process, effects.

"Or maybe I do and don't know it."

To paraphrase: one should not explain. One should never explain. Or, to tell is to show and tell. He prefers, we have seen, demonstration. Enactment. Directly and indirectly, thank you Mme. Burroway.

"Watching hard work is hardly working, but I can't help myself."

Too easy.
"She's all man."

RIGHT.

Oh—and the big man's mother hailed originally from Puerto Rico, sí.
"Tierra."

This is important. Kinda.

And there should be a dog in here someplace, a small collie, belongs to Wylie. "Champion."

This is not so important. But audiences will be pleased.

"We must attend to our critical literature."
And have a handbook handy. Say, *The Harper Handbook to Literature.*

"Used to be, myth was to realism what abstraction was to representation. Thus myth, with irony [itself a distancing effect], becomes a way out of the solely representational in *Ulysses*, even as cubism challenges realist geometries.

"Used to be. *Ulysses* today is no longer viewed as an 'abstract' work—it's now regarded more as a reworking of mythical coordinates to accommodate a reinstantiation of the real, the flux of the real.

"Thus myth will henceforth carry a union card, QED."

All cribbed, cursory.

That what you had in mind?

"My, but he's a self-made man."

Or a manmade self (this be not new). Ergo, manmade self-made man? Or simply a made man?

Never mind. Clever is as clever does, albeit auteurs needs must, on occasion, work out their problems in the full light of authorial day.

To hammer it home, see, for instance, Mississippi John Hurt's "Spike Driver Blues."

Not a mirror up to nature, as Brecht put it, but mirroring nature.

Let's get real then, leave the mirror stages, imagine a way to imagine.

Rule of threes: The Man is to The Wager as The Wager is to The Myth. Autotelic in some respects, then, a template in others. A high-concept B-movie, you might say, animated. Form follows gumption, "never more than a *revelation* of content," she (a poet) avowed. If you let it, could be a "gumption trap" too, as—what's his name, the motorcycle guy put it.

But let's not get too neoclassical, either, especially not with a minute a page at stake. At least. Space is time is money, which may or may not have anything to do with art, but has everything to do with commerce. And let's not get too *Homo economicus* about our manual labor, or work, or whatever Arendt would have wanted it to be, sodbuster.

"Gonna get colder before it gets hotter."

One can only hope.

"I am race, race I am."
"I am care, care I am."

Only in America.

"I want to live in."

Only in America?

All the livelong day.

~

Since so much fiction today borrows from a specifically cinematic template, we will pursue that correspondence forthwith.

First, some advise that a (conventional) second act in today's B.O.-fixated industry requires three or more turning points, or reversals of fortune. (Some would distinguish between such terms perhaps too rigorously.) And third acts, as any good dramaturge will tell you, require that an unseen complication emerge just when the audience thinks everything is OK, or not OK.

Following is an attempt to provide a summary of the action commensurate with this rather demanding logic of reversals upon reversals:

1

We learn that Joe is vacillating in his commitment to a working-class life, and that this has implications for his relationship with Frannie.

2

We learn that Red has it in for the big man, and is plotting to undermine the big man's growing popularity at Atlas via some sort of wager.

3

We learn that the big man may be a draft dodger, and that he has taken a liking to Joe, and that Joe has pondered the size of the big man's dick.

4

We learn that Joe has some measure of literary talent, according to his mentor Mr. Loomis, who, we learn, is an acid freak; and we learn that the name "Perkins" will prove a clue of sorts to a mystery of sorts that may or may not be "solved."

5

We learn that this novel or novella (hereafter NON) evidently requires for its elaboration the reflexive incursion of literary-theoretical material in order to foreground fully (and materially) the various and sundry motivations of authorship. Or to put it another way, we learn that this NON might have (creaky) autobiographical origins, and that its occasional appeal to authenticity, much like its appeal to racial strife and gendered inequalities, is counterbalanced by a cleverness that smacks at times of academicism.

Or to put it another way, we learn that the backstory relating to the conception of this NON is a vital aspect of the (at bottom) pulpish, high-concept conceit that this NON attempts to enact, and further, that this conceit will be enacted with due regard for the potentialities of the written word, regardless of the implications for possible future adaptation and (conceptual) appropriation.

Or to put it another way, we learn that this NON refuses to deny the legitimacy of the mythical or the representational or the cliché even in the face of postmodern traditions, hence it might be understood as a modest attempt to straddle the (waning?) aesthetic divide between high realism and experimental prose, and those persistent discrepancies animating the trade (literary fiction) and avant-garde fiction markets. (As has been attempted countless times in the past. Note that these latter binaries of uncertain half life operate as the fission products of a detonated modernism, a modernism intended, in its more radical configurations, to detonate culture itself.) Or to put it another way, we learn that this NON may be viewed as a work of (combustible) postmodernism that has abandoned several of the key tenets of same, and in so doing has revealed itself as the atavistic contribution of a poet who thinks he's a novelist who thinks he's a poet, and is angling in any case for a modest advance, regarding which self-publication online via _____ will almost certainly render said poet-novelist-poet a poor fisherman.

6

We learn, or should learn, that no attempt will be made to gesture toward an autonomous art form, that words are as corruptible as flesh, and that commercial interests abound throughout.

7

We learn, or should learn, that adapting this work for the screen may prove to be more difficult than anticipated, in light of which the adaptation currently making the rounds is apt to have a tough go of it.

8

We learn next to nothing about Debussy and his *Lepidoptera*.

9

We learn that a good night's sleep and a good bowel movement are essential to a good day's work under the sun.

10

We learn that less is sometimes more, and that more is sometimes less.

~

But lo, we're still *in* the second act, two-thirds of the way through the would-that-it-were high-concept whole, and some of us would like to imagine that a modicum of suspense has been maintained throughout, that our dear co-conspirators (i.e., readers) might yet find themselves, tentatively at least, on the edge of their proverbial seats. As you totter together on this edge, that habitual form of passivity draws near once again, incumbent upon escape—onto other such edges, suspending other such spans. Let us not amplify the problems of interface, then, as we should be grateful for mere attention, and for the attentions of those who would trespass against us.

(Amen, brothers and sisters.)

If this be telescoping, yet there be madness in 't. Besides,

"Narrative sense, narrative power can survive ANY truncation" (*ABC of Reading*).

Another kind of wager, goes way, way back.

~

Your kind indulgence, please:

Of all the changes in American life brought by the Cold War, the most important by far, in my opinion, has been the vast diversion of energy and resources from the creative pursuits of a civilized society to the conduct of a costly and interminable struggle for world power.

And again:

This is not to suggest that intellectual, artistic and scientific excellence has been abandoned in our country. On the contrary, it is being pursued by more people with more energy and more striking results than at any time in our history.

And again:

But the pursuit of excellence and creativity remain the occupation of an elite segment of our society.

And finally:

I do not think we can avoid the conclusion that, despite a broadening interest in the arts, the level of popular taste in America remains far below what it can be, what it ought to be.

Thus for Sen. J. William Fulbright (D-AK), speaking at Chapel Hill, NC, in April 1964, the US is beginning to resemble "a honky-tonk of continental proportions."

~

1958 Rolba System Model R-40, distributed as an American Snowblast machine. 4-speed gearbox, 35 horsepower Volkswagen engine. Throw: 100 feet max. Weight: approximately one ton.

But that's one honkin' machine, don't you know. The most powerful walk-behind blower in this neck of the woods, possibly the most powerful in the Northeast at the time.

~

To wit: Red aims to pit the big man against Atlas's big blower. He's willing to bet even money that the blower can throw more snow in less time than the big man can shovel—he knows that *no man* can throw that much snow that fast—and Red figures that, in addition to breaking the budgets of his mules and pocketing a tidy little sum for his trouble, defeating the big man in the light of day will put an end to the back talk he's been getting, the small acts of defiance that have grown more frequent with each of the big man's exploits. Work output is as high as ever, maybe even higher, but the men are learning to help one another with their duties, which takes some of the edge off of the more backbreaking work. And Red's blood boils at the sight of his mules behaving like men.

News spreads around town of Red's wager, and before long Mannville's shops and factories are all abuzz with talk of the coming Atlas trial. To cover himself, Red explains his rationale to Mr. White, whose response is typically laissez-faire.

–Whatever you say, Red. You're the man in charge, and I pay you to do what you have to in order to keep our little enterprise in the black.

Now, anyone who's known Red has, sooner or later, bumped up against his ornery side. There's a shared sense among many in town that the former jarhead—who, to secure his reputation as a tough guy, has found it expedient to lie about seeing combat in Korea (only his wife knows that he popped a hernia stateside)—is long overdue for his comeuppance. And yet most are aware of how brutal Red can be, to what lengths he will go to make a point or to gain some personal advantage. Red has in fact gone to considerable lengths this time out, betting each man at Atlas a week's pay that his machine can beat the big man. Even though Red's paycheck is a third again that of the next highest paid man at the garage, this means that his end of the bet amounts to a month's salary. Seen from his perspective, Red's is not a small gamble for a man with four mouths to feed.

But to Red's way of thinking, the gamble is as imperative as the stakes are high: either he wins this bet or his mules might decide collectively to tell him where to get off. After all, they know that he knows he can't fire *all* of them. Even White wouldn't stand for that level of disruption.

To his men's way of thinking, Red's challenge has begun to feel much like a matter of survival. Looking Red straight in the eye with a defiant glare has given them a small taste of autonomy, animating their workaday lives. They now feel as if they have a *say* in what goes on at Atlas. They now feel as if their work has *meaning*. They now feel they're a part of something bigger than themselves, a daily revolution of the spirit.

Thus far all of this has taken place, however, without anyone having thought to approach the big man to see if he even cares to participate in Red's wager. It's been tacitly assumed that Ant would be more than happy to fight the good fight, to sacrifice his brawn at the altar of the majority's betterment. Obviously someone needs now to approach him, so the men at Atlas discuss it among themselves, and Joe volunteers to make the pitch.

But what Joe and the other men don't know is that Red never intends for there to be a contest as such. He knows that *no man* can throw snow as fast as the big blower—and he trusts no one but himself to be the walk-behind operator—but he's not one to leave things to chance. Men as bitter and as fearful as Red make not one move without a little insurance. Machines, after all, have been known to break down—even with the expert going-over Red will have Shorty give the blower, with Red overseeing Shorty's every move—and there will be no rain checks on this wager: as Red had Buster set the terms, the machine and the man show up on the appointed day at the appointed hour, or they don't. If either party doesn't show, the other wins the bet, period.

Period.

~

While all of this is going down, the big man has, again, taken young Joe under his wing, as they say. This will prove the basis for the logline:

```
A  tough  laborer  shows  a  young  man  the  ropes  as  the
Vietnam War escalates.
```

(Replace "tough" with "strong" or "superhuman" depending on marketing climate. A more active logline might go something like:

```
When a strong laborer shows a young worker the ropes,
both find themselves pitted against a tyrannical
foreman.
```

Maybe we would do well to mention—no, too much on the nose.)

On this basis, and as some would have it, the author(s) would have done well to insert, midway through this act, the customary montage sequence: the big man showing Joe how to conserve his energies on the job; the two men working side-by-side with great efficiency; in all, a growing friendship. Several more intimate sequences would round out the relational themes: Joe introducing Ant, awkwardly, to his mother, and the three sitting down over tuna fish sandwiches and coffee; Joe introducing Ant, awkwardly, to Frannie, and Ant serving as something of an escort for the two during a night out at Mickey's, a drive to the park at the outskirts of town; and so forth.

One problem with the montage sequence and the additional material, however, is that readers will doubtless have expected them. Another problem is that this is a literary work, whereas the screenplay to be derived from this work will likely be a different beast altogether, at least insofar as visualizing what, on these pages, owes not a little to formal kinetics.

Nevertheless, the big man *has* taken young Joe under his wing. He *has* had lunch with Joe and his mother, in fact—tuna melts, with hot chocolate for the big man, the three discussing Joe's father, his desire to see his son succeed in life; and he *has* escorted Frannie and Joe to the park, and to Mickey's one night, leaving early to drive back to Rome when it becomes all too evident to the three that his presence in the bar is well-received only by Wylie and Charlie. Before he leaves, however, the big man manages to communicate to Frannie his love for his wife Jesse.

–Don't know where I'd be without her.

He also manages to exchange a few words with Frannie about Joe attending college.

–That's what I've been trying to tell him too, Antonio.

The two are of one mind, then, in wanting to see Joe do better with his life. Again, Joe is the kind of guy people pursue.

In addition to the home and park and bar sequences, the big man, day by day, does in fact show Joe the tricks of the shovel trade—how, for instance, to take some of the burden off of your biceps and triceps by using your weight to your advantage.

But more importantly, the big man begins to wean Joe *off* of such work, debunking the glories of a lifetime of manual labor.

–By forty your back'll be shot, by fifty you'll be walkin' all stooped over, by sixty you'll be one foot in the grave. Like my daddy. Mulework's no life fo a kid with a head on his shoulders.

And sometimes—not always, but sometimes—he lets Joe know where he stands, in no uncertain terms, on pressing social matters.

–But don't you think it's our duty to serve Uncle Sam, Ant? That's what my father did when he was my age.
–My daddy too. But depends whatcha mean by "serve." Ain't right for nobody to do somethin' wrong just because everyone's doin' it. The war you and my daddy fought in, that was a different kinda war.
–You mean you think this war is wrong?
–It's a white man's war, kid, usin' white men and black men to kill yeller men. Way I figger it, Uncle Sam's got his reasons, but I don't figger they're any good. So I want no part of it, neither should nobody with a head on his shoulders. Best to go to college and stay there till it's over.
–You telling me you're afraid of dying in combat?
–Ain't afraid of combat, I don't think. And ain't afraid of dyin', 'xactly. But I'm scared to death a throwin' my life away by killin' someone who doesn't need killin'. 'Sides, don't know what Jesse and her folks'd do without the money I send 'em.
–Does she have a job?

–Yeah, she cleans rich folks' homes. It's hard on her back and knees, but she's a strong young gal and it pays better 'n minmum.

–So what am I supposed to say to my aunt and uncle in Syracuse. My cousin Sammy's over there now, and—

–Listen, kid: pay no never-mind to what the relatives say. You get your ass off to college, you do somethin' with yourself. That's what I say, anyway. Each man makes his own bed, answers to hisself, in the end.

~

Joe, figured here as a real human being, may by story's end experience deep emotional, and possibly spiritual, transformation. The big man, a more mythic figure, may experience a new set of emotional attachments, while confronting something of a predicament, due to Red's scheming, upon which confrontation will hinge the resolution of the action; otherwise, as a mythic figure, the big man must remain relatively static, inert.

But to assert as much is to treat this NON more as an allegory—of human versus mythic nature, for one, but also, at another level, as an allegory of narrative itself (and narrative cinema)—than as a stage for human characterization, which it aspires also to be, mythical overtures notwithstanding. We would not deny our work its debt to eighteenth-, nineteenth- and twentieth-century precursors. Whether any character, conceived as a flesh and blood character, exhibits some essential or universal human trait is, in our view, a judgment best left to the reader (and in the screen version, viewers will likely respond as much to the living presence of actors as to anything we might have them *say*).

If there are surprises in store for readers or viewers, then, these will likely emerge not from any particular stylistic or narrative (or filmic) innovation, but from the simple juxtaposition of the conceptual-mythic and the concrete-mundane—which itself represents a minor if nontrivial departure from the dictates of conventional realist narrative.

~

Prospective screenwriters, take note: the Madeleine-Perkins-Loomis thread might be rendered as flashback, or (our recommendation) may be dispensed with altogether, the better to ensure a taut storyline.

~

OPENING CREDITS

White screen, silence. Then the muffled impact of snow falling against snow, gradually augmented by the rhythmic grating sound of someone shoveling. The white screen slowly reveals contrast, then the flickering texture of snow appears and the vague contours of the shoveler can momentarily be seen hunched over at his work, his shovel striking deep into the snow to hurl it to the side. This image fades as the rhythmic grating is gradually muted and replaced by the muffled impact of snow. The screen slowly returns to whiteout, and silence.

What happens at the skin is more like than different from what happens within.

Charles Olson, "Human Universe"

ACT III

The Myth

OPENING CREDITS

White screen, silence. Then the muffled impact of snow falling against snow, gradually augmented by the rhythmic grating sound of someone shoveling. The white screen slowly reveals contrast, then the flickering texture of snow appears and the vague contours of the shoveler can momentarily be seen hunched over at his work, his shovel striking deep into the snow to hurl it to the side. This image fades as the rhythmic grating is gradually muted and replaced by the muffled impact of snow. The screen slowly returns to whiteout, and silence.

FADE TO BLACK:

Written & Inspected by

J. Amato

FADE TO WHITE:

9

Shoptalk

Editor's is a steady rumble, voiced over and under the real. She's the talk in my sleep these days. And she's there for a reason, she tells me: to set the record straight.

~

Mannville has a small law enforcement outfit—three officers, two cars, with assistance as needed from the county sheriff's department and the State Police. The small town is well below the state average for all criminal activities, but Mannville cops see a fair number of weather-related fender-benders during the winter months.

Red is tight with one of the deputies, Odin. He and Odin have bonded over civil rights—more specifically, over the threat that the Civil Rights movement poses, in their eyes, to their hard-earned place in civilization's pecking order. For the past week Odin has, at Red's request, been checking with law enforcement officials in the city of Charleston and Kanawha County, West Virginia, and has phoned several federal agencies, in an effort to ascertain Antonio Lincoln's selective service status.

–You positive?
–Nigger's on the run, Red, no doubt about it.

Red and Odin have just seated themselves in a booth at Ruby's, midday. It's overcast, late in February, with snow in the forecast and hard-packed snow and ice on the ground, the kind of late-season day that even the most seasoned locals have a hard time greeting with a smile.

–What can I get you, Odin?
–Coffee, regular. And a club sandwich, Ginger.
–You Red?
–Black. And a grilled cheese, side of slaw. Not the mayo—the vinegar and oil.
–Be up in a minute.

Ginger disappears into the kitchen.

–So what do you want me to do, Red?

Red thinks for a moment, then leans back in his seat, the vinyl crunching as he shifts his weight. He puts his Chesterfield out in the ashtray to the side of the table.

–Nothing—not a goddamn thing.
–But I thought—
–Don't think. Leave the thinking to me.
–But aintcha gonna nail that nigger deserter?
–There'll be time for that.
–What do you mean?
–First things first. Looks like me and Jackson are gonna have us a little powwow.

~

Frannie and Joe are waiting for me outside of my house in Joe's old Pontiac. It's not too cold out, temperatures hovering just above freezing, the sun peaking through the clouds every half-hour or so just to be sure you know it's still there. I grab my hat and gloves, tell the folks I'll be back by dinner, and head out the door thinking I just *gotta* get my own place.

Today is Saturday, and since the weather is good and everyone is dog-tired, it's what Joe and I call a jerk-off day. Just Frannie, Joe and me, the odd wheel. But we're old friends, so we're comfortable with the arrangement.

We've decided to take a drive out into the country, for starters. We know where we'll end up later tonight—Mickey's—and we know too that, whatever we might imagine will happen, there's not a helluvalot to do in and around Mannville on a cold winter's day. So we figure we'll just keep moving, and if we're lucky, we might discover something new around the bend.

Joe and Frannie have picked up a six-pack of Pabst on the way over, and we each cradle one in our laps as we hit the old county route, eyes peeled for town clowns. The road slopes up and down and around, up and down and around, greens and browns occasionally poking through the white, a different vista opening at each dip or rise or turn in the road.

We pass Dean's old farm, the farmhouse itself boarded up now, and Frannie wants to get out and stretch her legs a bit. Joe pulls the car into the rutted driveway, and the three of us make our way around back to the hardscrabble field, now covered in snow and ice. I stop to take a piss up against a frozen birch tree.

Something pulls the three of us together across the field, the wind having drifted the snow to irregular levels, a few feet deep in some spots and a few inches deep in others. We zigzag across trying to avoid the deeper stuff, the beer frosting our insides. We reach a portion of the field that had probably flooded over sometime in early winter, maybe a foot deep and frozen solid until the past week's gradual thaw.

It's just a few hundred square feet of frozen-over earth, the sort of improvised space we might have tried to skate on as kids. Upon which we might have forgotten about the passing of time, the passing of all things. As we walk out on it and stand, together, Frannie's hand in Joe's and mine curled around my beer, our combined weight fractures the surface slightly. Below the surface we can just make out some liquid movement. But we continue to stand there together, the three of us, staring out at the surrounding woods, wondering what's next. What can be next.

~

—So that's the deal then?
—That's it.

The two men stand facing each other in the garage, one smoking, the other with a shovel over his shoulder just long enough to span the distance that separates them. Shadows across faces, smoke from the cigarette curling up and around. It's late. Only two vehicles are parked out front, the big man's wagon and a red Dodge pickup.

—What's to stop me from telling the guys what you're up to?
—Go ahead—open your big mouth, big man. You'll do time—serious time, my deputy buddy tells me.
—That so?
—That's so.
—And since I won't be able to face off against you and your blower next week—
—Your "friends" will lose their hard-earned wages, that's right.
—And you don't think they're gonna see right through this?
—Makes no fuckin' difference what they see through, boy. If you no-show, I win, plain and simple. But—

Red pauses, takes a drag off his Chesterfield.

—But I'll tell you what: as long as you don't tell no one about our little transaction here tonight, I won't blow you in—and I'll promise not to take your friends' money. You not showin' up'll just sting their pride a bit.
—Just their pride.
—That's right.
—And if I show?

—You show, my machine'll whip your black ass, your friends'll be halfway to the poorhouse, *and* you'll end up in the joint. You've got everything to lose and nothin' to gain by showin' up.
—Nothin' to gain. And I'm just s'posed to trust you?
—That's right. You ain't got no choice.
—Man's always got a choice, I s'pose.

The big man glances down as he says this, then stares at Red.

—That all there is to it then?
—Nope, not quite: I don't wanna see you around here after your no-show, got that? I want your black ass gone.
—You firin' me?
—If anyone asks, you can tell 'em you were laid-off.
—Laid-off?
—The weather's gonna be easing up soon anyway. So you'll just have to find another way to support that squaw you keep back in that West Virginia shantytown.

There's iron in the big man's eyes now as he stares at Red, methodically lifting his shovel from his shoulder and setting the edge squarely on the concrete floor before him. He clutches the handle tightly with both hands, one on top of the other, knuckles bulging like turnips. Red's body wavers a minute amount, throwing him off-balance. He catches himself with his left foot, but after a moment or two musters a defiant posture, the big man having fallen utterly silent, peering deeply into the black and white of Red's one eye.

~

—Can't do it, Joe.
—Why not, Ant?
—Just can't, is all.
—It's that fucker Red, isn't it?
—
—You didn't cut some kinda deal with him did you?
—
—What's wrong, Ant?
—Next Thursday'll be my last day on the job, Joe.

–What? You mean––
–I mean next Thursday's it, kid.
–And you're not even gonna––but what about the bet?
–Nobody's gonna get hurt on that.
–Ant, I don't think––
–Listen, somethin' you gotta know 'bout me, kid, 'cause sooner or later you gonna hear some talk.

~

It's true, Frannie and I were waiting for Wylie outside of his house that day. As I recall, though, he'd forgotten his hat and gloves in his rush to leave the uncaring quiet of his home.

Had to give it the old college try, as Loomis used to say. Had to make Wylie as focal to the story as he actually was. He was there all right, nearly every day.

But Wylie, poor Wylie, he couldn't last the stretch. Frail and awaiting my arrival, he'd asked me to finish the job. He'd asked me to, and I said yes. He was gone the next day. That's the long and the short of it.

~

Wylie had said nothing about his project in the letter that appeared in my mailbox, out of the blue, not a week before the funeral. The envelope was addressed to me in a familiar cursive. It took me a few moments to recognize the handwriting. It was Frannie's.

That old flood of bitterness hit me in the gut again––feelings I hadn't felt in years. When they subsided, I realized that I'd been little more than a fool to let my correspondence with the two dwindle to a yearly Christmas card with "Joe" scrawled at the bottom. That Frannie and Wylie would end up together should have been clear to me from the moment I left Mannville for college.

For another world.

~

I knew the news would be bad. In his letter, Wylie had given me to understand that he didn't have long, that he wasn't strong enough to travel, and that he wanted to see me one final time. My professional self couldn't help but detect a touch of the poet in the letter's matter-of-fact understatement of the inevitable—poets know when to hold back—and this caught me by surprise, I must confess, as I'd always figured Wylie for a sentimentalist at heart. The next day I was on a plane headed east.

I landed at Hancock Airport in Syracuse and rented a car. The flat, wooded vista along the highway north, subdued by a thick luster of white, put my mind at ease. Oneida Lake was iced over, and in the distance I could just make out a small troupe of stalwarts waging war with hockey sticks in a remote corner not far from the shoreline.

It had been nearly two decades since I'd last set foot in my place of birth. The day was cold and overcast, familiar February weather, and I parked in downtown Mannville. I'd heard about the factory closings, but with the exception of a new coffee shop, the town didn't seem to have changed much, mercifully. I half expected to bump into someone from the past—Charlie (she'd long since left Mannville, daughter in tow, for points unknown), Dean (he'd passed away years ago), Mr. Colella (ditto), Mr. White (Alzheimer's), Red (rumor had it he'd relocated to Phoenix with his family), even the big man—but I knew this was just geography speaking through the fibers in my body that it had helped to shape. I walked the few blocks to my mother and father's gravesite, resting my hand for just a moment on the frosted marble headstone, and then walked back to my car to drive to Wylie and Frannie's small house on the edge of town.

Save for a slight hitch in her walk from a bad fall she'd taken the winter prior, Frannie still exuded that same earthy charm of bygone years. She was greying now, like me. We hugged for a minute without speaking.

I was stunned at first to learn from her that Wylie had been writing for so many years, for so many years trying to get those times, those magical times, just so, writing and rewriting even after the factory closings, even while working one dead-end job after another. Frannie led me into Wylie's wood-paneled den. The writing itself—what Wylie had called his "manuscript"—was spread out over an old wooden desk: fifty or sixty failed starts of five and ten word-processed pages apiece; a dozen journals, each with a half-dozen entries; scraps of paper covered with illegible notes; dozens of computer files, most of which contained two or three sentences; in all, but the fragments of a writing life.

Some of the fragments were good, very good. But Wylie just hadn't been able to put it all together, to stop sweating the small stuff and put that matter-of-fact style of his to the straightforward task of relating what happened. He got too caught up in his method, I think, in those stacks of craft-based books that littered his workspace, books that can overwhelm anyone with their how-to advice.

What he needed to know had less to do with technique or with style than with *purpose*—with never losing sight of what he was trying to accomplish as a writer, and why. I could have helped him stay the course, if only he'd asked.

If only I'd been in touch.

Wylie had a real knack for details, for the odd observation, often scribbled in haste on a small scrap of paper. Occasionally something he'd written would jolt me back to 1965 in all its bittersweet glory. The big man had, it seems, figured large in both of our reckonings of that time, as if in tribute to the memory of our tribe. There was an impenetrable mystery about it all, or perhaps it was merely that we had grown too much to understand what had actually happened, time providing us with perspective at the expense of impression.

~

I braced myself as Frannie led me into Wylie's bedroom. He was a little guy, stood all of about five-three, weighed maybe one-thirty soaking wet. But he was a scrappy little fucker in his prime, and loyal to a fault.

Wylie's eyes brightened when he saw me, and he held out his hand.

–Joe.

The guy was all skin and bones, and I hugged him where he lay. We had about two hours together, two hours to fix our friendship for eternity, two hours during which we did what old friends do: we reminisced about old times. Toward the end of our time together, the discussion turned toward the manuscript. Wylie had no illusions about his own writing efforts. "It's not much, what I've managed," he sighed, "but it's something." He made me promise to "just write it all up as it happened," and use his work however I liked. He said he wanted my name and my name alone on it as author—"it'll sell better that way," he said. "And besides," he added, "you oughtta get something out of traveling all this way to see me. For being such a good friend."

Such a good friend.

The next day he was gone.

~

After the funeral, a frozen affair with six people in attendance, I began to pick through Wylie's accumulated writings. At some point he had begun working on some crude sketches, apparently entertaining the idea of an illustrated presentation of some sort. While never much of a draftsman myself, it seemed to me that the story, a clash of black and white amidst shades of grey, cried out for visualization.

The next day the idea came to me that a novel or novella could be served up schematically, without the customary machinery of description and emplotment. Not a series of vignettes, exactly, but an extended treatment that would include suggestive feints at incident and character. A tired idea as soon as it materialized, maybe. But as I look back on it all now with another century's hindsight, from the moment the big man entered the scene it was all cinema passing as reality anyway. What better way to prepare a prospectus for the film that would unreel those workaday passions?

And it would be easier to sell the screenplay with a novel or novella behind it. I was doing OK financially, but Frannie could use the money. So why not?

Reading over Wylie's "manuscript" wasn't easy for me. It wasn't easy for me to learn that he'd evidently put so much stock in my doing something important with myself. I must have failed him then, I think, as all I have to show for the past thirty years is a pile of newsprint and three stories that went national. Not even any kids.

But I won't fail him now.

~

Some will chalk up this book to survivor guilt, finally, but it's not about getting things out of my system. Writing has never been, for me, therapy or raw experience or self-expression, however therapeutic or raw the experience or expressive the outcome. I don't know how Wylie felt about this exactly, but to judge by his efforts, faltering or no, he was after something more than self-help or simple representation or sheer expression. Or potboiler. Or for that matter, *chef d'oeuvre*.

Some will observe that the whole amounts to a self-indulgent improbability. Self-indulgent, possibly; improbable, probably. But I've followed Wylie's lead as much as I was able, and I have a good idea, thanks to Frannie, of what he thought about *me* in particular back then. So pardon me if I write about myself, intermittently, from his point of view. Unreliability may result, as I may have sacrificed a measure of objectivity. But I'm no less truthful for all that, and readers will have gained some additional perspective by permitting Wylie to be as Wylie ended his life—a writer.

~

Wylie was inside out and outside in. He was who he thought he was, the real deal. His only mistake was a conscious one: trying to do the work that *I* should have been doing, me and my sheepskin and all. To tell what happened so many years ago, to tell it like it was *and* like it might have been. He may have been thinking about Frannie, too.

~

I never got a chance to tell Wylie—I only discovered this about myself when I began to read through his writing—but I envied him his realism. What he envied in me, I think now, was what he took to be the dreamer in me. But all of these years, my writing has never been imaginative. Not until now.

So I guess you could say it took Wylie's realism to bring out the romantic in me. And the romantic in me decided to type the manuscript using the tool I'd used when first I learned that the alphabet would keep me out of the Mannville woods: Loomis's trusty old Underwood Touchmaster V, his gift to me when I entered college.

I'd have to locate ribbons first; it wouldn't be easy after sitting at a keyboard for so many years, cutting and pasting with abandon; and it probably wouldn't make for a better read in the end. But the extra manual effort required to pound down each letter, to write and revise slowly and painstakingly—call me a fool, but this somehow seemed the labor appropriate to such a labor of love.

And to hear as much is bound to satisfy those who prefer more discipline and more brawn. But after all, writers only do what they gotta do, and I needed to find a way to link the alphabet as I knew it then, fresh and beckoning, with the alphabet as I've come to know it, beat-up and worn down by the grinding commerciality of so much public discourse.

~

The big man would have told me to conserve my energies, put them where they matter most—in the words themselves. But I'm my own man now.

~

Still, some will be disappointed in us, Wylie and me. So many readers have come to expect the screed of a single heart's struggles. So many will want more to hang onto, more to read into, more to trudge through, more to *read*. Wait a moment while I get out my onomasticon....

Rest assured, the story is all here.

~

And Editor?

Fuck her, as Wylie would say.
Fuck her if she can't take a joke.

~

Thing is, it was no laughing matter: it was Wylie who went off to war.

Me, I got the deferment. The chance. The chance to dream.

Him, he went, he came back. But he never had a chance, not a chance at all. Never could be the same man, or the man he could have been. Frannie did what she could for him, as he did what he could for himself.

So this is Wylie Packard's doing, this book. The words are mine—a few lines, but only a few, lifted as-is out of Wylie's failed starts—and I'm the author, as Wylie would have it. As author, I take full responsibility for the book's execution. But it was Wylie, poor Wylie, who put me up to it, who lent the project its imprimatur, its horse sense.

Frannie—Frannie tells me that I'm doing right by Wylie, handling matters in this manner. She says some things need closure. In the past few days, the two of us have come to terms with much of what happened so long ago, and since, and why. Maybe this is the best one can hope for.

Best or no, it's what it is.

~

–So that's it then?
–That's right, that's it, old-timer.

–Well I don't see it that way, Red.

–You don't, huh?

–No, I don't. *We* don't.

–"We" don't? So all of a sudden a fuckin' milkman and his plow-jockey pals know more than I do about this business? I give an order, I expect you all to hop to it.

–But me and the boys—Charlie here too—we don't think you're being fair, Red.

–That a fact, Shorty?

–Yep, that's a fact.

–Yeah, that's right.

–Yeah.

–Lookie here, Red—no reason to put just two men on a load like that. We oughtta be able to give one another a hand. It's only fair.

–Fair, the man says. What about you, Charlie—you think it's only fair?

–Bet your ass, Red. That's too much lifting for just two guys. No reason for it.

–What I say goes, that's reason enough.

–Not anymore Red.

–Not anymore?

–We'll take it to White if we have to.

–I suppose I gotta eat this shit now from some two-dollar stick-in-the-ass blowjob?

–Watch your mouth Red.

–Who the FUCK do you think you are Red?

–Wylie! Joe!—I can handle this bastard myself.

–So now the little faggots are growing balls too?

–Back off, Red!

–Come here, bitch—

–Charlie! Charlie!—you OK?

–Yeah—yeah, I'm—I'm all right.

–Red you no good piece of sh—Ant!

–Ant, let him go!

–Let him go, Ant!

10

Outsourced

Q: If it's no fun for you, can it be fun for them?
I: Not likely.

Q: What is the function of Mannville's landscape at the present time?
I: (1) To assign value to the constellations. (2) To appeal to our devotions.

Q: What happens to Red?
I: The big man catches his wrist as he's about to backhand Charlie a second time, pinning Red's arm against a workbench with one hand and gripping Red's face with the other, forcing his head back and suffocating him, Red punching and kicking the big man to no avail and, finally, crying out for help. Joe and Wylie and the other men struggle to pull the big man off of Red, but it's Joe who persuades him finally to let Red go. Roughed up some and still catching his breath, Red straightens the patch over his eye, and shouts at the men "This ain't over, not by a long shot." He glares at Ant and storms out of the garage, Buster tagging behind.

Q: Who do you think you are?

I: The Ghost of Christmas Past, which is to say, of Modernism Yet to Come. The scrivener. The sound track. A member of the Gene Lockhart Fan Club. Master Factotum. Someone's alter ego, once removed. The score. A (secular) critic. An archaism. All three first persons' second or third person. An analog device, possibly the camera. An outlet for the author's frustrations with conventional narrative. Just another style. A differential function. A postmortem mood, outmoded. The machine in the ghost in the plot. A collective bargain. More gratuitous print matter. A demigod. A calculated risk. A loss of control. The sign of excess. An ode, elapsed. A panegyric, overtaken. No—I mean panjandrum. So, a mistake, made new. A check on the annalic. *Not* one of Le Sueur's "work heroes." A composer. The miniaturist litany composed by a composer. The argument Fate, made good. A she-devil. A shooting draft. A freak of nature. The interviewee. Racial equality, resexed. Another purveyor of another Magical Negro. POV, sampled and remixed. A bluff. Your amigo, hombre. The answer.

Q: What is the significance of being left-handed?
I:

Q: What is the key reversal of the third act?
I: The big man's entirely predictable decision to damn the torpedoes and match himself against Red and his blower. It all happens very quickly, the sequence of events roughly as follows:

First, Charlie overhears Buster at Mickey's boasting to Stan about how he and Red have got the big man "by the short hairs," how "there won't even *be* a contest." Stan is upset because, like a few other local outfits, Baum's has its own parlay going and he's covered three bets on the big man himself. "I coulda won some serious cash with Red and that blower a his," Stan complains, adding that the men at Atlas are "gonna be good and pissed once they learn their jungle bunny ain't a showin'." Buster assures Stan that "me and Red won't be asking anyone to make good on their bets—we're not out to hurt the guys." Stan is impressed. "That's mighty white a you two." "Well," explains Buster, "we just wanna make sure they know who all's in charge." Buster grins, Stan nodding his head in approval.

Charlie phones Joe, and the next night—the Wednesday before the big man is to work his last shift—Joe, Wylie and Charlie convene an eleventh-hour meeting with Shorty and Dean at the factory parking lot. It's a cold clear night, moonbeams illuminating the surrounding snowscape. POV JOE as he, Wylie and Charlie approach Shorty and Red. Joe explains to the two men that the big man is a draft dodger, and that Red has figured this out. ANGLE ON Shorty, himself a veteran, who's clearly not pleased to hear about the big man's draft status. Charlie, holding a bundled, sleeping Sally in her arms, next relates what she's overheard: that if the big man no-shows, Red won't ask the men to make good on their wager. "So the bastard is out to show us for once and for all who's boss," concludes Shorty. "If we let him get away with this, the whole town'll hear what a helluva guy he is." "And after that roughing up he got the other day," Dean surmises, "I figure Red'll use Ant's sudden departure to prove to White that he needs even more free rein with us." "One more thing you gotta know," adds Joe. "Ant has a wife back in West Virginia who's cleaning houses to make ends meet." "So then it's like this," says Charlie: "if Ant wants to do right by himself *and* by his family, he no-shows." ANGLE ON Shorty, deep in thought. ANGLE ON Joe, then Charlie, then Wylie, who exchange nervous glances with one another. "But what about doing right by his country?" Shorty asks. "You sure going over there *is* doing right by our country?" Dean asks. CLOSE ON Joe, who looks especially concerned.

The next morning the big man turns into the Atlas lot, surprised to see all of the Atlas workers—Joe, Wylie, Charlie, Dean, Shorty, Carl, Gus, Lucas, even White's two nephews—standing outside of the garage, hands in pockets and huddled together. Red hasn't arrived yet. As the big man gets out of his car, Joe approaches him to say that the men believe, to a man, that he can beat the blower, and that they're still willing to wager their paychecks, their livelihoods, their pride by betting on him. "We all know that if you go up against Red and his machine, you're gonna have to quit Atlas—maybe even quit New York, maybe even the country," Dean begins, "but we figure—" CLOSE ON the big man, who finishes Dean's thought. "You're right, I know it—the man's gonna blow me in no matter what I do." Ant pauses.

134

"But you guys—you guys gotta know," Ant says, "draft or no, I'da showed to beat that son of a bitch if I'da thought you was all willin' to bet on me." The men cheer and embrace the big man as they walk inside the garage together.

When Red pulls up to the garage minutes later, his face and neck still bearing the imprints of the big man's large hand, Dean walks out to meet him. "Just so you know," Dean says, proudly, "and *all* the guys are in agreement: the contest is *on* this Saturday and Ant ain't going *nowhere* till then. So you call off that town clown friend of yours or we'll let White know what you been up to. I'm sure he'll be pleased as punch to hear that his top dog's been betting against his hourlies." Red tips his head back, jaw jutting out and teeth locked in a defiant grin "Yeah? I got news for you, milkman—White knows all about it, and he don't give a shit." If he's surprised to hear this, Dean doesn't show it. "Is that so? Well then, I can think of a few other things he might wanna hear about." "Yeah? Like what?" "Oh, like how you been using *his* workers and *his* equipment to clear *your* aunts' and uncles' and cousins' driveways." "White's got too much goin' on to give a rat's ass about that," Red snarls. "You sure about that, Red?" Red thinks about it for a few seconds. "OK—you and your asshole buddies have it your way then. You're even more stupid than I gave you credit for, bettin' on that dumb coon. But I'll be more'n happy to take your money."

Of course, none of this is as we would prefer to have related it. But as they say on-the-job, *it'll have to do*.

Q: Do you have anything to add before we retire you?
I: For one, we would have preferred a more elaborate presentation of the circumstances surrounding the big man's decision to avoid the draft. The intervening years have rendered the ethics of such a decision rather more clear-cut than they were at the time.

Also, something along the lines of the following:

"To the best of our knowledge, not a soul in Mannville heard from the big man again after the Saturday of the showdown, though there were rumors to the effect that he'd crossed the border into Canada. Some insisted that he'd ended up in Southeast Asia, and ended up a casualty, but his name appears nowhere on The Wall in DC. Others believed he'd eventually made his way back to West Virginia, and to Jesse. All of the people whose lives he'd helped to change believed pretty much what they wanted to believe. All, that is, except Joe, who'd go silent whenever someone speculated as to the whereabouts of the big man.

"Think of the short novel as a long poem. Think of the smells and tastes of the working classes, and pause to consider whether and to what extent what is called 'the examined life' may be conditioned by such smells and tastes. Make an effort to understand how outside becomes inside, how a paycheck becomes a foodstuff becomes a pattern of belief. Thus you wind up at some very old news.

"When summer finally arrived, Joe dreamed the dandelions in Frannie's back yard produced a wine with 'real legs,' the term Mr. C. used in jokingly describing his Pink Catawba. Now Joe, you see, he loved a plate of eggs and potatoes for supper, but he knew nothing at all about wine. So he decided to find out."

11

Debriefing

If the matrimonial merger of a mainline debutante and a corporate magnate had not produced Madeleine Brandt, the publishing industry would have had to invent the pain in the ass. But she was at any rate an invention, forged through years of studied interpersonal frugality. And whatever Madeleine's late-career misgivings, however much she wavered presently from prior articles of faith, it seemed as if fiction itself required her type to attain its fictive ends. And these ends were about to draw her into an even more intimate engagement with the substance of her work.

According to Madeleine's Cartier, Perkins had been at the manuscript for all of thirty-two minutes, flipping through its pages and reading randomly to size it up as quickly as possible, when, to Madeleine's surprise, she abruptly set the document on the marble table, resolutely lifting the wine glass to her lips to drain the last sip of Sancerre, then dipping her head a few millimeters and smiling to herself ever so slightly as if to acknowledge a hard-won private knowledge.

—Well, Ms. Perkins?

—

—Ms. Perkins?

–Sorry Madeleine. Well—aside from the Hellenic, Homeric, and Norse overtures, not all of which work for me—
–Yes?
–And the scholarly apparatus, that myth-narrative stuff—perhaps too—too much abstruse material, and at the same time, not enough—
–Yes—what else though? You've read the story before?

Perkins dipped her head another millimeter, evidently deep in thought.

–Ms. Perkins?

Perkins knew Madeleine was now hanging on her every word, and she might easily have used this to some advantage had she a shred of interest in serving Madeleine her comeuppance for those countless meetings in which she'd been forced to endure the senior editor's irrepressible expertise in all matters editorial. But in point of fact Perkins *had* heard the story before, or more precisely, a semblance of it—as a child, from her grandmother—and she was hesitant to tell Madeleine her granny's story. For one, she wasn't quite certain that the story was hers to tell, but more importantly, she questioned the wisdom of giving up that much of *herself* to the pain in the ass. And even were she, out of sheer generosity, to opt to relate the story to Madeleine, where to begin? And how to explain to Madeleine that the version of the story appearing before her in these carefully manicured pages constituted a theft of somewhat greater moment than Granny's secondhand retelling?

~

–So you see, eventually Loomis put Granny Imogene directly in touch with his student, and the two struck up a correspondence that lasted till just before Granny passed. Weird pen pals—a white boy and a middle-aged black woman.

Madeleine fidgeted in her seat just enough to make the satiny smooth futon cover squeak.

–So you're telling me, what, that your grandmother just happened to know the author of a work submitted to her granddaughter's employer?

–Well, there *is* some coincidence at work here, but—it's a little more complicated than that, Madeleine. If you read the letters—
–The letters?
–Yes. Mom—my mom let me have the letters he sent Granny. They average about one every three-four months, for roughly thirty years. I have all but the last one, addressed to my mom—it's a eulogy that Mom read aloud at Granny's funeral.
–So what do the letters say?
–Well—

Perkins paused for effect, relishing this tiny affront to Madeleine's growing impatience.

–Well, it seems it didn't take him long to figure out that she was African American—Granny was awfully fond of talking about *her* granny, who was a slave in South Carolina.
–Anything else?
–They swapped notes about the arts, too. Granny was a devotee of so many arts—writing, music, theater. But especially writing. She just *loved* the Beats.
–Goodness knows why. Anything *else*?
–Otherwise the letters are pretty much what you would expect from a student, cub reporter, and eventually, an award-winning journalist. At first, mundane details about his college life, then the news about his jobs, eventually about his accomplishments, and so forth. Aside from his national rep as an investigative reporter—
–Well, I for one have never heard of him.
–He worked mostly for leftist outlets.

Madeleine arched her brows.

–Anyway, all pretty much standard letter-writing fare, except—

Again Perkins paused, Madeleine scooching forward to the very edge of her seat.

–Except what, Ms. Perkins?
–Well—

Suddenly Perkins's cell, which she had stuffed inconspicuously into a magazine rack between her chair and the futon, started playing a few bars of Glen Campbell's "Wichita Lineman." Perkins continued to address Madeleine as she reached over to retrieve the phone.

–Excuse me, Madeleine. I've been waiting for a call from a friend whose car has broken down to see if she needs me to take her grocery shopping tomorrow.
–That's quite all right.

Perkins muted the sound on the phone as she took a moment to see who was calling. Then she quickly composed and sent a text in reply, placing the phone back in the rack.

–Sorry Madeleine. I like crossover country. Especially the old stuff.
–The old stuff, I see. You were saying?
–Well, for starters, each and every letter Amato posted to my granny either refers directly or alludes to those six or seven weeks when the big man was in Mannville. It's as if he never entirely got over that time, even after he'd made a name for himself. It's easy enough to piece together the narrative just from these references, which is what Granny must have done.
–So?
–So think about it: Granny regaled me with the story as she'd been given to understand it, in bits and pieces, along with her—I guess the best word is *embellishments*. She called the story "Red Versus the Big Ant," and my sister and I, when we were kids, we used to plead with her to tell us what we called just "Big Ant." Granny used to tell my mom the story too, but Mom never fancied herself a storyteller, so she always deferred to Granny. In Granny's version, the big man wasn't AfroLatino, he was just bl—
–What does all this have to do with the manuscript?

Now it was Perkins's turn to appear irked.

–OK, go on, go on.

—Well you see, my sense is that this guy Amato was just a little obsessed with the story—kinda like my sister and me. Anyone who'd known him, even casually, would likely have heard about it. And would have picked it up, made it theirs. Just like Granny Imogene.

—Which explains why he wrote it up, right? He was a journalist, after all, and—

—I have a hunch it was too close to him. And reportage can be a way of getting *outside* of oneself—you of all people should know that.

—So what are you saying, Perkins?

Perkins's face beamed inadvertently this small victory.

—Well—

—Well *what*, Perkins?

—I'm saying that there is no way that the man who wrote Granny those letters authored this manuscript.

—You mean—

—I mean quite simply that the Joe Amato who authored this manuscript—

Perkins lifted the manuscript from the table, holding it aloft in her left hand.

—is not the same Joe Amato who lived in Mannville circa 1965.

~

—And all of this on the basis of a single letter?

Perkins was now seated right beside Madeleine on the futon, both women ogling a yellowing, handwritten letter that Madeleine held in her right hand, her left now wrapped around a wine glass—red wine—to match the wine glass in her host's hand. A half-empty wine bottle sat on the table before the two women, flanking two colorful serving plates, three cheeses nestled on one—a pepper Boursin, an aged cheddar, Port Salut—the other with an assortment of crackers.

–You see, Amato signed each and every letter to Granny as he signed this letter—"Joseph," which is the name he went by as a journalist throughout his career. And yet the manuscript and cover letter are both signed "Joe." And in this one letter—

–He mentions his *other* pen pal, the doppelganger he befriended in college.

–Right. "My college buddy, Joe Amato"—the Joe Amato from Denver. Plus, he never mentions Wylie, or Charlie, or anyone else in *that* Mannville.

Perkins gestured toward the manuscript on the table.

–So—

–So Joe stole the idea from Joseph? But this would mean—

–This would mean that the coincidence here, and it is indeed a real coincidence, is that Joe submitted his work to Kletterkraft, without knowing that someone in Kletterkraft's employ, me—

–Had heard the story from her granny—grandmother, via Joseph—

–We can't be one-hundred-percent certain. But it's a good guess. For that matter, when you think about the type of work we've been acquiring over the past few years, it seems only natural that he'd give us a try.

–We *have* been leaning toward the sensational, that's true. And yet the details about Mannville, the snow—

–You know as well as I, Madeleine, that a good scribe can fake that sort of thing. Just takes a little research coupled with a little imagination. But who knows?—maybe his family hailed originally from Upstate. There are so many Italian-American families in that neck of the woods, and with the unemployment there and the weather—

Madeleine fidgeted in her seat.

–But anyway. All we can be sure of, assuming our Joseph here wasn't hallucinating, is that the big man arrived in Mannville circa 1965 to work with Atlas, and that such and so events transpired to lead to a contest between man and machine, a contest that may well have become part of the lore of that region. That much is in the letters, the rest is anyone's guess.

Madeleine placed the letter on the table, and scrunched her face as if put-upon by this newfound knowledge.

–But Perkins, don't you think that he, Joe, would be at least somewhat concerned that, once published, Joseph might get wind of—
–That possibility occurred to me, and it's what makes me think that much of the story is pure fabrication—Wylie, possibly, Frannie, probably. To judge by the cleverness of the whole, Joseph is enough of an auteur to pull off that much, I think. And of course we know that there was an Augustine Loomis, else—
–Else you and I would be fictive creatures!
–Naturally. And we know that Mannville is a real place. So we know that the man had a good deal of raw material to work with, whether secondhand or no we can't say. First things first, though: do we like the story enough to publish it?
–I think so, yes. It's overworked in spots, and there were a few places when I was afraid he was going to launch into a disquisition on silence, absence, contingency, the solitary soul yearning for its *raison* under the existential sun yadda yadda yadda—
–Yes, I felt that too at times. The occasional nudge toward Beckett, but only a nudge. A hint of the carnivalesque, but only a hint. The work is uneven, ragged even, perhaps deliberately so. And then there's the metafiction to consider—a bit dated at this point. And that argot.
–But the story's got heart, finally, and you know what Heine said about writing for the masses. So yes, I like it enough to publish it.
–That makes it unanimous.
–So then: what about possible legal complications?
–Here's the thing, Madeleine: let's say the story is all hooey. In which event, we're safe, because there's no law covering the theft of previously unpublished hooey.
–OK.
–Now let's say, on the other hand, that the story is based on fact. What's the harm in going with a second-hand retelling?
–We'd have to get him to change the names and such, just to be safe. Possibly set the story in another region of the US, someplace else with an Upstate. Pennsylvania, maybe. Illinois?
–Granted. Then all that's left is the ethical question: is it right to publish someone else's story without first asking their permission?
–That might be a question that only Joe can answer, but—

Madeleine sipped her wine, for the first time savoring what her highly refined taste buds told her was an excellent vintage.

–But personally, Perkins, I think not. It's possible too, I suppose, that Joe *did* ask for permission. Note the single initial "J" after that "Written and Inspected by" bit. Just a wee bit sly. Maybe too sly. And this *apparent* discrepancy between the manual Underwood copy mentioned in chapter nine and this here fancy-schmancy production—

Madeleine tipped her head at the manuscript resting on the table.

–It's almost coy.
–That's how I read it.
–So then: what we are asking our firm to publish is, in essence, a memoir or perhaps nonfiction novel in which the putative memoirist, Wylie—who is with us, incidentally, for only a short period *as* memoirist—
–Yes, that bugged me.
–Me too. So—Wylie the memoirist is revealed ultimately to be a fabrication of the author, Joe, an author who—and without this letter—

Madeleine picked up the letter and held it between her thumb and forefinger, wiggling it as she spoke.

–Without this letter, readers will really have no way of grasping this— an author who is himself passing as the story's original narrator, Joseph.
–Well—yes, yes, provided Joseph Amato can be called the *original* narrator. Surely there are other narrators, you know. If there's any truth to it whatever, I imagine this story has become pretty popular in the Mannville area alone.
–Doubtless you're correct, Perkins.

Madeleine set the letter down, and the two women contemplated together the age-old prospect of an endless string of such tales transmitted across landscape and generation.

—You know, Madeleine, it occurs to me that we *could* contact Joseph Amato ourselves—

—But why?

—Simply to check out the story, to see if there's a grain of truth to it.

—Fact checking? We're not journalists, Perkins.

—Of course you're right.

—Besides, if it *were* to turn out that Joseph is in the process of writing up *his* version—

—You mean, as related in the manuscript, after Wylie's death—

—Yes. What if Joe has in fact stumbled upon Joseph's intentions, whether by accident or because Joseph has told him—

—Then by contacting Joseph—I mean, assuming the man is still alive— we jeopardize our editorial neutrality, and we risk losing a damn good yarn, one that has option written all over it.

—Precisely. Amato is clearly aware that it doesn't really matter how he handles the form of the story, or what medium it's presented in. Beyond the modest talent and discipline it takes to compose a work of fiction—

—Yes.

—Well, craft is somewhat beside the point in this case, I think. Given the mythic oomph he's tapped into, he could put the story out there with a semaphore and it would still find its audience. Eventually, I mean. Just look at how I learned of the story. In fact—

—What?

—I'm thinking this might be the perfect opportunity for us to launch the ebook imprint that marketing has been going on about. Put it up on the Web and see what we hook by way of response.

—What an intriguing notion, Perkins. I rather like it.

Each woman took a sip from her wineglass. Perkins reached for a butterfly-shaped rye cracker.

—But you know, I'm thinking—this "treatment" idea I can tolerate, Madeleine, but *too* much self-reflexivity, and—

—I couldn't agree more.

—And then there's this Editor thing—and gendered male, of course.

—Naturally. But what do you suggest we do about it?

Perkins nibbled on her cracker.

–Well—hmm, let's see. Once we take the book we could always lean on him some, let him know that he really ought to be concentrating, first and foremost, on maintaining readers' interest. You know—keeping to a tight narrative line. I mean, this would seem to be what he's really after anyway.
–We wouldn't want him to sacrifice his guiding vision, though.
–What do you mean?
–He strikes me as a writer who feeds off of his digressions—this is what keeps his writing alive.
–His voice, you mean?
–Not just his voice. I mean the sense one gets about him *as* a writer—where he's coming from, the assumptions he brings to his work, consciously or otherwise. I get the distinct impression that this writer *needs* to turn his narrative inside out—to use his term—and I don't believe he'll take kindly to our interference.
–Hmm, I see. Shoot.

Madeleine and Perkins slumped back in their seats, putting their wineglasses to their lips in unison. Suddenly Perkins lurched forward, sliding her glass onto the table.

–Wait!
–What?
–There *is* another possibility, I think.
–Proceed.
–It's possible that, despite Amato's grab-bag approach, there's actually something *missing* in the text, something that might strengthen his treatment of authorship as such.
–Something missing?
–Yes—*us*.

~

–I think you can handle this then, Perkins?
–No problem.
–I have a hunch he'll be amenable to the idea once he learns that Loomis and your grand—granny were close friends.
–Even if he's not the Joseph Amato who studied with Loomis?

—Assuming there's even a smidgen of honor among thieves—

—Hmm, yes, you're probably correct, under the circumstances. He of all people should appreciate the personal history at stake here. Enhancing that history should make for an irresistible subplot, especially for a writer who, as you say, feeds off of his digressions—

—And has already toyed with the idea of editorial mechanism as a collaborating presence. At any rate a positively brilliant idea, Perkins.

—I think I'm going to prod him a bit too about this male gendering stuff. Lord knows he—or at least, his narrator—could stand a more hip sensibility in this regard.

—*Hip?*

—Hip.

—OK, as you wish. But I daresay you'll probably have to work rather closely with him to get this off the ground. Come to think of it, I had a similar experience when I was just starting out. I—but this can be an *awful* lot of work, you know.

—Not a problem. And thank *you*, Madeleine—the idea wouldn't have occurred to me without your insight.

Madeleine smiled a grateful smile. It lasted all of two seconds before she scrunched her face.

—One thing is still bothering me, though.

—What's that?

—All of this still doesn't explain why I feel like I've read this story someplace before.

—I don't know if I can help you there, Madeleine. As I say, it's likely that a number of us from Upstate have been walking around with versions of this story for years now.

—True.

—And word of mouth works in mysterious ways. Heck, maybe there *is* a published version of it in some small press journal. Plus—

—Plus what, Perkins?

—Well, one thing it's got going for it is that playful quality that you find in tall tales. I think most readers will automatically relate to it on that level.

—Right.

—And you know, we never did address what's probably the most obvious thematic element.

—What's that?

—You know—the steel-driving man motif.

—Oh, yes, the steel-driving thing. I'm afraid I wasn't quite sure what that was all about.

—Oh, Madeleine.

—What?

—Madeleine—

—*What?*

—My dear Madeleine, if you don't mind my saying so—

Perkins drew a deep breath, exhaling as she spoke.

—You can be *such* a pain in the ass.

Perkins smiled, a mischievous twinkle in her eyes, but a warm smile nonetheless. And after the obligatory look of outrage had crossed Madeleine's face, she managed in response, for the first time in a long while, an expression approaching genuine gratitude. If the evening would end on the somewhat pat note of newfound mutual respect, both women would be reminded many times, in the weeks and months ahead, of just how difficult it can be to negotiate, professionally, the terms of such rapport, even while working together to bring into print a tall tale that wrestled with the question of keeping to one's kind. But as luck would have it, both women knew, deep down where it hurts, that art could only ever approximate life, and this somber lesson in aesthetics kept their chins up until Madeleine's retirement fifteen months later, when Perkins was appointed her successor. The two never fell out of touch, and they reminisced often about the story that broke the ice.

12

Revelations

Prelude

Thus the fable, and filler, about two women trying to get a handle on a myth—the myth of authorship. A masculine myth, or a myth of masculinity?

[Insert twang.]

Either way, presented here for those with children, who want to believe that publishers can be so—generous? Imbibing? What comes next is for those without kids—a *really* big show. And it can happen only *once*—recount it again and again, as you wish, but the originating event is irreversible, nonrenewable. Thus is the world emptied of myth, thus is myth the action of a world emptying itself of myth.

Notes of a neolithic novelist: because the place, the times were manly, the myth would be manly, manly women would labor as long and as hard as manly men. And harder, and longer. That's right—*women*. This we have been at some pains to demonstrate. The main event is not man against machine, not really, for we would tell no tale of industrial revolution or "the great unwashed." We would ask you to consider instead a small revolt in the service sector.

Not hand-to-hand, customarily, yet head-to-head, mano a mano.

Shovel or machine, you work with the tools of the trade. To mediate musculature, to move atoms of snow and soil and soul alike. It's been said. A simple shovel renders the world a place to be unearthed, transported, metaphorized. It's a constitutive mediation, an authentic calculus for the hands holding the shovel, but is the tool an extension of the man, or vice versa?

Dig that pilcrow, sd Joe. *That DIY productivity.*

~

Hey, that's a managerial line of reasoning, old fellow, and a jive question for those who are forced, hour after waking hour, to square off against a regulated real, a real that takes its toll on you coming and going.

You need to get your hands dirty. You need to know shit from Shinola, your ass from a hole in the ground. You need the broadest palette, with just the right amount of gravitas.

~

You think you can take the measure of a man?

Think again. Of sweat, of calluses, of cells strengthened only to be damaged by railing too hard and too long against gravity and time and the elements.

You think you can take the measure of a machine?

Think again. Of fuels that translate to more digging and prying beneath the surface. A blower automates the manly bargain, converting fossil into horsepower, making of manpower a sideshow. Most of the time. And we need these machines to do the backbreaking work, the work that breaks backs, because we need more workers to do the work of living, of making life more livable for men and women alike. The work of finding new machines, machines that will make life more livable than the old machines. Machines made like men.

You think you know what it means to put another man down?

You figure it out. Just be sure to put down this book. And eat your Wheaties.

~

The result, which viewers will be sure to grasp as the film reaches its climax, would seem to be more property for a handful of planet-wide enterprises that want ever more property, intellectual property included.

Count me in.

And out.

~

Besides, a strong response does not necessarily a strong work of art make.

They say no one can know what it's like to fill another's shoes. But some come closer than others to that kind of knowledge. That kind of knowledge isn't learned—it's earned.

I read that someplace.

~

AND what of divergent myths, the appropriated and refigured stoicism of an Atlas (say) vis-à-vis those manufactured, overheated variants proffered by your beloved narrator, he (as we've verified) of covertly sincere, if overtly smartass, designs?

(With "designs" one might consider, too, the possible ramifications for qualia. And the $1000 subvention that should have helped bring this book into...print?

(How much materiality can you stand? How much *real*?

(And rest assured, apropos of the divergent, that we will attempt to forgo yet another myth of the state as we mount our Promethean resolution. Ditto church, albeit

what say ye to hymnography [say], via Sicily? Too cute perhaps? If the shoe fits....)

~

      Q1: If labor = text, does talent = metatext?
      Q2: If labor's gone local, has talent gone global?
      Q3: Can you diversify your way out of progress?
      Q4: Can you?
      Q5: When the robotic outstrips the human, what mythical place will mortality occupy in machine consciousness, and what will happen to our two-handed ~~mythologies~~ prostheses?
      Q6:
      Q7: An economy of innovation for an innovative economy?
      Q8: And the greater good?
      Q9: What of the greater good?
      Q10: Can mystery obtain in the very absence of mystery?

~

Does that make nine or ten?

& another Q: Are the stabs at docudrama a futile attempt to delay the onset of artifice?

Don't answer that.

&—this scrap comes suspiciously, if conspicuously, late, a conclusion suggested, some would say spuriously, by conceptual transposition:

If, as above, less may be more and more may be less, then no less than a midlist title may amount to little more than a self-published trifle.

Still, you never know. Maybe Mannville is a moveable feast?

~

Right: those of us who came up through the ranks—we don't play fair and square, ysee, and don't we know it. We'll use whatever we can to get our points across: a sledge, pyrotechnics, a [yawn], a rider, a still, a tin ear, JFK's "great enemy of truth" (1962, at Yale), two parallel lines that converge in the distance. A kick in the balls. A high carbon footprint. The feminization of knowledge work. *Écriture flying trapeze.* Karaoke. Magnets.

Even, dear lord, your cooperation.

Tough. Sue me, us. Him. If you're still with us, *this* machinery is the star you've hitched your wagon to. What gives—as the Gloucester poet might have put it—*trajectory.* That prepositional glue of life and limb and loss that fixes relation. That you follow, that you have to follow, to the end.

You just *have to.*

~

PRODUCTION END NOTES
FOR A WORKING-CLASS FANTASY

Plot & Character

Wylie's illness might be less literal than latent—loss of faith, boulevard of broken dreams; or could be tracked to Agent Orange, combat injuries, PTSD, etc. The story is Joe's and the big man's, and to a lesser extent Frannie's and Wylie's, so Wylie's struggles must exemplify the thematic commonplace of changing fortunes. Wylie could become the weak link, to be preyed upon by Red. Or simply eliminate such complications altogether to winnow the story down to its essentials.

Add dimension to Red's villainy. Make him a bigoted born-again? A loyal family man?

Complicate the big man's heroics. Served time for manslaughter? Make him brooding and introspective initially, but in contradistinction to the novel, show him to be surprisingly knowledgeable about, say, marine life, or an expert in hagiography, or poetry. An autodidact. Whatever else, mitigate the stereotype of the strong, silent, ingratiating black man.

Final disposition of the big man's shovel? And shouldn't it have a name? (Lucy?)

Can the action be moved ahead to the Christmas season, to make BIG MAN a holiday release? Can a snowball fight or two be incorporated into the action?

While adding dimension to characters, be sure to winnow the story down to its essentials.

Casting

Non-bodybuilder in the role of the big man.

Joe: sturdy type, just this side of handsome.

Wylie: must elicit sympathy.

Red: Ernest Borgnine forearms. Does not have red hair.

Frannie should radiate that earthy, ooh la la quality. But not a beauty per se.

Writer's Wish List

Above-the-line budget > 20 mil; location shooting (Central New York); original score; *no voiceover*; minimal digital effects. (Watch that scene in DeMille's *Samson and Delilah* where Mature as Samson insolently and effortlessly bends the spear. Study the reaction shots of Lansbury, Wilcoxon, and Lamarr.) Understate the superhuman/mythic/folkloric aspects of the story. Emphasis on how the extraordinary can inhabit the ordinary.

Attachments

None to date.

Merchandising

Hardware line; toy hardware line; action figure; sport wagon line; (graphic?) renovelization for YA market; "BEAT THE BIG MAN" video game; BIG MAN hot chocolate drink; BIG MAN Burger. (Note product placement in the novel, Gatorade in particular.)

Misc.

Sequel? Prequel? HBO series? *Second Life* estate? Update action to present day? (Swap draft for stop-loss etc.) If big budget: performance capture, 3D, full transmedia branding of franchise, and a story winnowed down to its essentials. If MOW: still image montage and/or animated action sequences, and a story winnowed down to its essentials.

Or just go with straight-up animation. See Caveat, below.

Works Cited

"Available upon request."

Caveat

Please note that reflexive aesthetics need not translate to cinema verité, found footage, etc. Whatever the production values, don't be afraid to say something without worrying too much about optics.

~

Sing, you sons of bitches, of that Saturday in March
in the bright morning sun
along the ridge near the park, at the outskirts
where Atlas black met Atlas white
where bragging rights meant human rights—*sing!*
of the good and proper fight.

Half the town turned out to see the tourney
the big man going eye-to-eye with Red
to clear a path a hundred long by three feet wide
under the deepest of cerulean skies, some said
with so much on the line, snow, cash and pride
the machine would leave the man half-dead.

The snow was waist-high, a little heavy
from the thaw, and when the big man pulled up
in his wagon, don't you know
some who would later bear witness whispered
their doubts, visible in the frosty air, that even such as he
could manhandle Red and his machine. And Buster snickered.

Lifting from the wagon's back his shovel, the big man
spotted Odin's car across the way
and as the Atlas men approached him, in a group
he shook each hand, then turned
away to take the full measure of the sun, of the air
of the land. Of the day.

Then he turned to Joe and
tipping his head at the cop car
said: "Me, my days are numbered, kid, but you—
you got a chance to go far." And with that
Joe, Wylie, Charlie and he, they say, climbed
the slight grade to the top of the ridge.

Red, Chesterfield in mouth, faced a throng of his own
as he fired up the '58 Rolba, shifting the machine into first
and it snorted and kicked like thirty-five mules, his backers
backslapping, yelling ugly epithets of race
as Red muscled the blower up the ridge, Buster
mustered into service as Red's second for the duel.

The big man stood silent and motionless
his hands clasped around the oak handle. Before him
staked out in the bright morning sun
gleamed his hundred-by-three-foot rectangle. His cohorts
confirmed terms with Buster as Red wrangled the Rolba
into place, its jerry-rigged Stars and Stripes shuddering.

"Whoever clears his path first, wins."
No heats, and brute force alone to ponder
and Charlie stands between the two men's lots—
yonder lies their icy feat, and fates—
and Charlie takes her gloves off, holds them high
but just before she lets them go to start the race

the big man slowly lifts his iron shovel
with his left hand, holding it vertically aloft
for just an instant
as if in tribute to the firmament.

(And let's keep in mind
that it's 1965 in Mannville, New York.
We want to be certain to provide an accurate context
for our impressions.)

And Charlie's gloves fall through space
to grace the snow, and you watching at this instant know that
contest, competition, tourney, race
trial, duel, match, or fight
this is to be a daylight journey
through have versus have-not might.

When the blower hits the snow it growls
and the ton of machine throws pound after pound of white
thirty yards west, Red scowling to maintain control
but the big man's shovel strikes six times, each fifty-pound
shovelful tossed a good sixty yards east
a total weight this rate of automation cannot best.

And Red pushes harder, his forearms bulging
man and machine again neck and neck, but the big man shovels
harder still, throwing the snow now a hundred feet up, up
and away as if by sheer will, and the townsfolk, in awe
follow the arc of shoveled snow as it glistens
blindingly in the bright morning sun.

Ten yards in, and Red shifts into fourth, pushing
the Rolba for all man and machine are worth
his Chesterfield dropping from his lips, for an instant
the machine inching ahead, tuned by Shorty within an inch
of its life—but in that instant and across that inch the big man shovels
        harder still
as if by sheer will, hurling the snow hundreds of feet up, shattering air

and the well-tuned blower begins to choke on the load, gears grinding
and the townsfolk follow the arc of the big man's heave
and the snow glistens blindingly, and most turn away
and the machine growls a final time
twenty yards in, and stalls
and the big man continues to throw the snow

now a thousand feet up, and Red stands, staring
at the blinding display, helpless in the face of such
hands, such heart, such will
and he watches the shimmering crystals of white
dancing freely against the blue, shovel ringing out
its contents—You sons of bitches have been there too, *sing!*—

and Red's retina takes it in, and in
too much light for any mortal eye

and Red's vision will die on the day
that the big man comes to the end of his labors
and what Red glimpses in his mind's eye then, who can tell?
but when he sees again it will be well into night.

And as Buster leads Red, poor rigid Red, back to his dejected pack
Mr. White pulls up in his black sedan
to be joined by Odin—who points, first, to the Rolba
stalled atop the ridge, then to poor snow-blind Red
and then to the big man, chief culprit in this public
spectacle of a business divided against itself.

You see, with White's authority to countermand Red's
orders, Odin figures he's free to nab the big man on his own
and the big man sees Odin with White, and sees
him pointing at him and him alone, and knows
it's either fight again, or flight, and decides then and there
it's time to hit the road.

And so, Wylie, Charlie and Joe, with Frannie at his side
near tears, escort the big man to his car
amid the cheers. And the big man faces Joe
a final time, his left hand holding Joe's right shoulder.
"They can break you, kid"
he says, and his words hit home like thunder.

"They can break you, kid," he tells him
and he leaves the town in wonder.

Epilogue

~

As Wylie's voiceover will likely serve as the framing device by which we learn of the story of the big man and Joe, we need now to return to Mannville, years hence.

~

It's Indian summer. Wylie—older, stockier, sporting facial hair and a tattoo on his left forearm—is leaving the baby food factory at the end of a long workday. He's asked by a coworker whether he'll be at Mickey's later that night.

–Not tonight, Rob. Maybe tomorrow night.

Later that evening, just at magic hour, Wylie turns his pickup into the park, and pulls up to the ridge where Red met his match. He gets out, Marlboro in hand and wearing a baseball cap, and coughs a few times. The man is clearly not in the best of health. An older Frannie gets out of the passenger side. They walk together to the top of the ridge, seating themselves side-by-side on the fading grass, hands clasped around their knees to watch the last rays of sun filter through the fall colors. They're silent for a few lingering moments.

–Won't be long before it snows.
–Summer was too short this year.
–What summer?

Wylie laughs, coughing.

–If only winter didn't last so long.
–Yeah. Yknow—

Wylie puts out his Marlboro by pushing the smoldering tip into the earth at his side.

–What's that, lover?
–Sometimes—sometimes I—

His voice trails off. Neither looks at the other. Frannie smiles—a sad smile—and huddles up tighter against Wylie. Both wonder what's next. What can be next.

FADE TO

ABOUT THE AUTHOR
THE PERSON WHO, AS WE ALL KNOW, WROTE THIS BOOK
AND WHO IS THEREFORE PROXIMATELY RESPONSIBLE FOR IT
HENCE IS THE PERSON TO BE CONTACTED REGARDING
ANY INQUIRIES, COMPLAINTS, OR PENDING LITIGATION

Joe Amato completed his undergraduate degrees in mathematics and mechanical engineering at Syracuse University, and his Master of Arts and doctoral degrees in English at University at Albany. A licensed professional engineer in New York State, he spent seven years in industry working in various project engineering capacities. Amato is the author of nine books: *Samuel Taylor's Last Night* (novel, Dalkey Archive Press, forthcoming 2012); *Big Man with a Shovel* (novel, Steerage Press, 2011); *Once an Engineer: A Song of the Salt City* (memoir, SUNY Press, 2009); *Pain Plus Thyme* (poetry, Factory School, 2008); *Industrial Poetics: Demo Tracks for a Mobile Culture* (criticism, University of Iowa Press, 2006); *Under Virga* (poetry, Chax Press, 2006); *Finger Exorcised* (poetry, BlazeVOX [books], 2006); *Bookend: Anatomies of a Virtual Self* (criticism, SUNY Press, 1997); and *Symptoms of a Finer Age* (poetry, Viet Nam Generation, 1994). With Kass Fleisher, Amato is the author of three award-winning screenplays and, most recently, a full-length play, *Fat Jack's*. Amato and Fleisher have also adapted *Big Man* for the screen. Amato currently teaches writing and literature at Illinois State University. He's easily tracked down via any number of social and surveillance networks.